W9-CLS-613

HBR'S
10
MUST
READS

On
Collaboration

HBR's 10 Must Reads series is the definitive collection of ideas and best practices for aspiring and experienced leaders alike. These books offer essential reading selected from the pages of *Harvard Business Review* on topics critical to the success of every manager.

Titles include:

HBR's 10 Must Reads on Change Management
HBR's 10 Must Reads on Collaboration
HBR's 10 Must Reads on Communication
HBR's 10 Must Reads on Innovation
HBR's 10 Must Reads on Leadership
HBR's 10 Must Reads on Making Smart Decisions
HBR's 10 Must Reads on Managing People
HBR's 10 Must Reads on Managing Yourself
HBR's 10 Must Reads on Strategic Marketing
HBR's 10 Must Reads on Strategy
HBR's 10 Must Reads on Teams
HBR's 10 Must Reads: The Essentials

On
Collaboration

HARVARD BUSINESS REVIEW PRESS
Boston, Massachusetts

Copyright 2013 Harvard Business School Publishing Corporation
All rights reserved
Printed in the United States of America
10 9 8 7 6 5 4 3 2 1

The web addresses referenced in this book were live and correct at the time of the book's publication but may be subject to change.

Library of Congress Cataloging-in-Publication Data

HBR's 10 must reads on collaboration.
    p. cm.
  Includes index.
  ISBN 978-1-4221-9012-8 (alk. paper)
  1. Business networks. 2. Cooperativeness. 3. Interorganizational relations.
I. Harvard business review. II. Title: HBR's ten must reads on collaboration.
III. Title: Harvard business review's 10 must reads on collaboration.
  HD69. S8H39 2013
  658'.046—dc23   2012037906

ISBN: 9781422190128
eISBN: 9781422191422

The paper used in this publication meets the requirements of the American National Standard for Permanence of Paper for Publications and Documents in Libraries and Archives z39.48-1992.

Contents

Are You a Collaborative Leader?   1
Herminia Ibarra and Morten T. Hansen

Social Intelligence and the Biology of Leadership   15
Daniel Goleman and Richard Boyatzis

Bringing Minds Together   31
John Abele

Building a Collaborative Enterprise   45
Paul Adler, Charles Heckscher, and Laurence Prusak

Silo Busting: How to Execute on the Promise of Customer Focus   59
Ranjay Gulati

Harnessing Your Staff's Informal Networks   79
Richard McDermott and Douglas Archibald

Want Collaboration? Accept—and Actively Manage—Conflict   91
Jeff Weiss and Jonathan Hughes

Shattering the Myths About Enterprise 2.0   113
Andrew P. McAfee

When Internal Collaboration Is Bad for Your Company   125
Morten T. Hansen

Which Kind of Collaboration Is Right for You?   137
Gary P. Pisano and Roberto Verganti

About the Contributors   153
Index   155

On
Collaboration

Are You a Collaborative Leader?

by Herminia Ibarra and Morten T. Hansen

WATCHING HIS EMPLOYEES use a new social technology, Marc Benioff, the CEO of Salesforce.com, had an epiphany. His company had developed Chatter, a Facebook-inspired application for companies that allows users to keep track of their colleagues and customers and share information and ideas. The employees had been trying it out internally, not just within their own work groups but across the entire organization. As Benioff read the Chatter posts, he realized that many of the people who had critical customer knowledge and were adding the most value were not even known to the management team.

The view into top management from the rank and file was just as obscure, Benioff knew. For instance, the company's annual management off-site was coming up, and he could tell from talking to employees that they wondered about what went on behind closed doors at that gathering. "They imagined we were dressing up in robes and chanting," he says.

What could he do to bring the top tier of the company closer to the workforce? Benioff asked himself. And then it hit him: Let's use Chatter to blow open the doors of the management off-site.

What greeted the 200 executives who attended that meeting was atypical. All 5,000 Salesforce.com employees had been invited to join them—virtually. Huge TV monitors placed throughout the meeting room displayed the special Chatter forum set up for the off-site. Every manager received an iPod Touch, and every table had an iPad, which attendees could use to post to the forum. A video service broadcast the meeting in real time to all employees, who could beam in and instantaneously express their views on Chatter, too.

The meeting began with the standard presentations. The managers watching them weren't quite sure what to do. Nothing unusual happened at first. Finally, Benioff grabbed the iPad on his table and made a comment on Chatter, noting what he found interesting about what was being said and adding a joke to spice it up. Some in the room followed with a few comments, and then employees watching from their offices launched a few comments back. The snowball started rolling. "Suddenly, the meeting went from a select group participating to the entire company participating," Benioff says.

Comments flew. "We felt the empowerment in the room," recalls Steve Gillmor, the head of technical media strategy.

In the end the dialogue lasted for weeks beyond the actual meeting. More important, by fostering a discussion across the entire organization, Benioff has been able to better align the whole workforce around its mission. The event served as a catalyst for the creation of a more open and empowered culture at the company.

Like Salesforce.com's managers and employees, businesspeople today are working more collaboratively than ever before, not just inside companies but also with suppliers, customers, governments, and universities. Global virtual teams are the norm, not the exception. Facebook, Twitter, LinkedIn, videoconferencing, and a host of other technologies have put connectivity on steroids and enabled new forms of collaboration that would have been impossible a short while ago.

Many executives realize that they need a new playbook for this hyperconnected environment. Those who climbed the corporate ladder in silos while using a "command and control" style can have a difficult time adjusting to the new realities. Conversely, managers who try to lead by consensus can quickly see decision making and execution grind to a halt. Crafting the right leadership style isn't easy.

Idea in Brief

Social media and technologies have put connectivity on steroids and made collaboration more integral to business than ever. But without the right leadership, collaboration can go astray. Employees who try to collaborate on everything may wind up stuck in endless meetings, struggling to reach agreement. On the other side of the coin, executives who came of age during the heyday of "command and control" management can have trouble adjusting their style to fit the new realities.

In their research on top-performing CEOs, Insead professors Ibarra and Hansen have examined what it takes to be a collaborative leader. They've found that it requires connecting people and ideas outside an organization to those inside it, leveraging diverse talent, modeling collaborative behavior at the top, and showing a strong hand to keep teams from getting mired in debate. In this article, they describe tactics that executives from Akamai, GE, Reckitt Benckiser, and other firms use in those four areas and how they foster high-performance collaborative cultures in their organizations.

As part of our research on top-performing CEOs (see "The Best-Performing CEOs in the World," HBR January–February 2010), we've examined what it means to be a collaborative leader. We've discovered that it requires strong skills in four areas: playing the role of connector, attracting diverse talent, modeling collaboration at the top, and showing a strong hand to keep teams from getting mired in debate. The good news is, our research also suggests that these skills can be learned—and can help executives generate exceptional long-term performance.

Play Global Connector

In his best-selling book *The Tipping Point,* Malcolm Gladwell used the term "connector" to describe individuals who have many ties to different social worlds. It's not the number of people they know that makes connectors significant, however; it's their ability to link people, ideas, and resources that wouldn't normally bump into one another. In business, connectors are critical facilitators of collaboration.

Play Global Connector

- Do you attend conferences outside your professional specialty?
- Are you part of a global network like Young Presidents' Organization?
- Do you regularly blog or e-mail employees about trends, ideas, and people you encounter outside your organization?
- How often do you meet with parties outside your company (competitors, consumers, government officials, university contacts, and so on) who are not directly relevant to your immediate job demands or current operations?
- Are you on the board of any outside organizations?

For David Kenny, the president of Akamai Technologies, being a connector is one of the most important ways he adds value. He spends much of his time traveling around the world to meet with employees, partners, and customers. "I spend time with media owners to hear what they think about digital platforms, Facebook, and new pricing models, and with Microsoft leaders to get their views on cloud computing," he says. "I'm interested in hearing how our clients feel about macroeconomic issues, the G20, and how debt will affect future generations." These conversations lead to new strategic insights and relationships, and help Akamai develop critical external partnerships.

Connecting the world outside to people inside the company is crucial to Kenny. He uses a number of tactics to do this. "First, I check in on Foursquare often and post my location to Facebook and Twitter," he says. "It lets employees in different Akamai locations know I'm in town so that anybody at any level can bring me suggestions or concerns. Second, every time I go to one of our locations, I have lunch or coffee with 20 to 40 people. We go around the room, and people ask questions on topics they most want to address. Often my answer is to connect them with others in Akamai or even people at other companies who have expertise on the topic. Third, if I see a big opportunity when meeting with a customer or colleague, I will schedule a follow-up visit and bring along the right experts from

Akamai. Fourth, whenever I travel, I try to make room to meet with two to three people I know in that location. Whenever possible, I bring someone else from Akamai with me to those meetings."

Kenny's networking recently resulted in an important strategic alliance with Ericsson. Akamai is now working with the mobile giant to change consumers' internet experiences on mobile devices. The partnership evolved out of a conversation Kenny had with a midlevel Ericsson executive two years ago at the Monaco Media Forum. "It really changed my idea of what Ericsson could be, and I saw that we were both trying to solve a similar technical problem," Kenny says. "Then I worked through mutual friends to meet their CEO and arranged for the right people on his team to meet with their Akamai counterparts."

Presidents and CEOs aren't the only executives building bridges between their organizations and the outside world nowadays. Take Beth Comstock, the chief marketing officer of General Electric. She is famous for her weekly "BlackBerry Beth" blog, in which she shares what she has learned in her external role for busy (and perhaps more internally focused) GE managers. The pithy and provocative blog goes out to thousands of GE's sales, marketing, and technology leaders. In it, Comstock passes along interesting information that people might have missed, taking care to tie it back to challenges and opportunities GE faces. For example, in a recent post from the World Economic Forum, she reported that a panel of scientists had come to the same conclusion that a GE survey had—that technology alone cannot ensure innovation and that more training in creativity is needed.

"I work hard to curate information that I don't believe many at GE will have heard and to translate information in a way that is relevant to our challenges," says Comstock. "I probably spend half of my time immersed in worlds beyond GE. I hope this encourages my colleagues to be more externally focused. The message is 'If I find it important to spend some of my time this way, maybe you will, too.'"

To connect their organizations to the wider world, collaborative leaders develop contacts not only in the typical areas—local clubs, industry associations, and customer and supplier relations—but beyond them. Networking in adjacent industries, innovation hot spots like Silicon Valley, or emerging economies or with people of different educational or ethnic backgrounds helps open their eyes to new business opportunities and partners. For example, Comstock's external contacts in the innovation space led GE to NASA, with which the corporation has shared insights and best practices. The two organizations have also begun discussions about space technologies that might have applications in health care.

Engage Talent at the Periphery

Research has consistently shown that diverse teams produce better results, provided they are well led. The ability to bring together people from different backgrounds, disciplines, cultures, and generations and leverage all they have to offer, therefore, is a must-have for leaders. Yet many companies spend inordinate amounts of time, money, and energy attracting talented employees only to subject them to homogenizing processes that kill creativity. In a lot of multinational companies, for example, nonnative English speakers are at a disadvantage. To senior management, they don't sound as "leader-like" as the Anglophones, and they end up getting passed over for promotions. At a time when innovations are increasingly originating in emerging markets, companies that allow this to happen lose out.

France's Danone, one of the top performers in our research, makes sure its executives don't encounter such obstacles. When all the managers worldwide get together for the company's annual strategic review, many choose to present in their native tongue. Says CEO Franck Riboud: "We spend a fortune on interpreters so that being less articulate in English is not a barrier. Some of our executives have even presented their business case in native dress. This helps us steal away talent from competitors where those who don't speak perfect English get stuck."

Reckitt Benckiser, the UK-based producer of home, health, and personal care products and another top performer in our research, considers the diversity of its workforce to be one of its competitive advantages—and a key reason it has seen net income grow 17%

Engage Talent at the Periphery

- How diverse is your immediate team in terms of nationality? Gender? Age?
- How much time do you spend outside your home country?
- Have you visited your emerging markets this year?
- Does your network include people in their twenties (who *aren't* your kids)?

annually, on average, from 1999 to 2010. No nationality dominates the company's senior team. Two executives are Dutch, one is German, two are British, one is South African, two are Italian, and one is from India. According to (soon-to-retire) CEO Bart Becht: "It doesn't matter whether I have a Pakistani, a Chinese person, a Brit, or a Turk, man or woman, sitting in the same room, or whether I have people from sales or something else, so long as I have people with different experiences—because the chance for new ideas is much greater when you have people with different backgrounds. The chance for conflict is also higher—and conflict is good per se, as long as it's constructive and gets us to the best idea."

As Becht suggests, nationality isn't the only kind of diversity that matters. Research on creative industries shows that the collaborations that are most successful (whether in terms of patent citation, critical acclaim, or financial return) include both experienced people and newcomers and bring together people who haven't worked with one another before. Leaders need to make a concerted effort to promote this mix: Left to their own devices, people will choose to collaborate with others they know well or who have similar backgrounds. Static groups breed insularity, which can be deadly for innovation. Nokia's former executive team, for example, was 100% Finnish and had worked closely together for more than a decade. Many believe homogeneity explains why the team failed to see the smartphone threat emerging from Silicon Valley.

Collaborative leaders ensure that teams stay fresh via periodic infusions of new players. Including employees from Generation Y—those born from the mid-1970s to the early 2000s, who have grown up sharing knowledge and opinions online—is another obvious way to enliven collaborations. A number of leading companies have begun using technology to harness Gen Y ideas and perspectives. Salesforce.com, as we have seen, brought them in from the periphery by using Chatter to open its management offsite to all staff. At India's HCL, employees throughout the company join virtual conversations on topics that are important to them, and CEO Vineet Nayar reaches out personally through a popular blog that allows him to interact with a broad cross section of employees. In a market where the competition for engineering talent is fierce, the ability to attract the best and brightest helped HCL grow 30% annually from 2008 to 2010.

Collaborate at the Top First

It's not enough for leaders to spot collaborative opportunities and attract the best talent to them. They must also set the tone by being good collaborators themselves. All too often, efforts to collaborate in the middle are sabotaged by political games and turf battles higher up in the organization. Consider that Microsoft, according to a former company executive writing in the *New York Times* last year, developed a viable tablet computer more than a decade ago but failed to preempt Apple's smash hit because competing Microsoft divisions conspired to kill the project.

Part of the problem is that many leadership teams, composed of the CEO and his or her direct reports, actually don't operate as teams. Each member runs his or her own region, function, or product or service category, without much responsibility—or incentive—for aligning the organization's various projects and operations into a coherent whole.

At Brazil's Natura Cosméticos, CEO Alessandro Carlucci has instituted a comprehensive "engagement process" that promotes a collaborative mind-set at all levels and has helped the firm win a top spot on *Fortune*'s list of best companies for leaders. The process was implemented after Natura's highly successful IPO in 2004, when

Collaborate at the Top First

- Do members of your team have any joint responsibilities beyond their individual goals?
- Does the compensation of your direct reports depend on any collective goals or reflect any collective responsibilities?
- What specifically have you done to eradicate power struggles within your team?
- Do your direct reports have both performance and learning goals?

competing agendas among the senior managers began to threaten the company's prospects. Carlucci decided he needed to reorganize the executive committee to unify its members around common goals and stop the power struggles. He asked the members of the top team to make a commitment to self-development as part of their stewardship of the company.

Each executive embarked on a "personal journey" with an external coach, who met with everyone individually and with the team as a group. "It is a different type of coaching," Carlucci explains. "It's not just talking to your boss or subordinates but talking about a person's life history, with their families; it is more holistic, broader, integrating all the different roles of a human being."

Roberto Pedote, Natura's senior vice president for finance, IT, and legal affairs, adds: "I think that the main point is that we are making ourselves vulnerable, showing that we are not supermen, that we have failures; that we are afraid of some things and we don't have all the answers."

Since the engagement process was adopted, Natura's executives have become much better at teaming up on efforts to improve the business, which grew by 21% in 2010. The collaborative mind-set at the top has cascaded down to the rest of the organization, and the process has been rolled out to all the company's managers.

If leaders are to encourage more innovation through partnerships across sectors and with suppliers, customers, and consumers, they need to stop relying heavily on short-term performance indicators. According to the psychologist Carol Dweck, people are driven to do

Collaboration Does Not Equal Consensus

COLLABORATIVE LEADERSHIP IS THE capacity to engage people and groups outside one's formal control and inspire them to work toward common goals—despite differences in convictions, cultural values, and operating norms.

Most people understand intuitively that collaborative leadership is the opposite of the old command-and-control model, but the differences with a consensus-based approach are more nuanced. Following are some helpful distinctions between the three leadership styles.

tasks by either performance or learning goals. When performance goals dominate an environment, people are motivated to show others that they have a valued attribute, such as intelligence or leadership. When learning goals dominate, they are motivated to *develop* the attribute. Performance goals, she finds, induce people to favor tasks that will make them look good over tasks that will help them learn. A shift toward learning goals will make managers more open to exploring opportunities to acquire knowledge from others.

At HCL, CEO Vineet Nayar demonstrated his commitment to collaboration by adopting a radically different 360-degree evaluation for his top managers—one that invited a wide range of employees to weigh in. Although the company had done 360-degree reviews before, each manager had been assessed by a relatively small number of people, mostly within the manager's immediate span of control. As Nayar recalls in his book *Employees First, Customers Second* (Harvard Business Review Press, 2010), "most of the respondents operated within the same area as the person they were evaluating. This reinforced the boundaries between the parts of the pyramid. But we were trying to change all that. We wanted to encourage people to operate across these boundaries." Nayar set the tone by posting his own 360-degree evaluation on the web. Once executives got used to the new transparency, the 360-degree reviews were expanded to a broader group. A new feature, "Happy Feet," was added, allowing all employees whom a manager might affect or influence to evaluate that manager—regardless of their reporting relationship.

Comparing three styles of leadership

	Command and control	Consensus	Collaborative
ORGANIZATIONAL STRUCTURE	Hierarchy	Matrix or small group	Dispersed, cross-organizational network
WHO HAS THE RELEVANT INFORMATION?	Senior management	Formally designated members or representatives of the relevant geographies and disciplines	Employees at all levels and locations and a variety of external stakeholders
WHO HAS THE AUTHORITY TO MAKE FINAL DECISIONS?	The people at the top of the organization have clear authority	All parties have equal authority	The people leading collaborations have clear authority
WHAT IS THE BASIS FOR ACCOUNTABILITY AND CONTROL?	Financial results against plan	Many performance indicators, by function or geography	Performance on achieving shared goals
WHERE DOES IT WORK BEST?	Works well within a defined hierarchy; works poorly for complex organizations and when innovation is important	Works well in small teams; works poorly when speed is important	Works well for diverse groups and cross-unit and cross-company work, and when innovation and creativity are critical

Depoliticizing senior management so that executives are rewarded for collaborating rather than promoting their individual agendas is an absolute essential. At Reckitt Benckiser, there's little tolerance for politics. Says Bart Becht: "We go out of our way to make sure that politics get eradicated, because I think they're very bad for an organization. I think they're poison, to be honest with you." Becht's direct, no-nonsense style and the expectation that people should openly disagree with one another in meetings also help keep politics to a minimum, allowing real teamwork to take hold.

Show a Strong Hand

Once leaders start getting employees to collaborate, they face a different problem: overdoing it. Too often people will try to collaborate on everything and wind up in endless meetings, debating ideas and struggling to find consensus. They can't reach decisions and execute quickly. Collaboration becomes not the oil greasing the wheel but the sand grinding it to a halt.

Effective collaborative leaders assume a strong role directing teams. They maintain agility by forming and disbanding them as opportunities come and go—in much the same way that Hollywood producers, directors, actors, writers, and technicians establish teams for the life of movie projects. Collaborative efforts are highly fluid and not confined to company silos.

Effective leaders also assign clear decision rights and responsibilities, so that at the appropriate point someone can end the discussion and make a final call. Although constructive confrontation and tempered disagreements are encouraged, battles aren't left raging on. This is exactly how things work at Reckitt Benckiser. When teams meet, people know that it is OK—in fact expected—to propose ideas and challenge one another. They debate loudly and furiously until the best idea wins. If no obvious agreement is reached in time, the person chairing the meeting normally makes a decision and the rest of the group falls in line. This ensures vigorous debate but clear decisions and quick action—diversity in counsel, unity in command, as Cyrus the Great once said.

Loosening Control Without Losing Control

In the old world of silos and solo players, leaders had access to everything they needed under one roof, and a command-and-control style served them well. But things have changed: The world has become much more interconnected, and if executives don't know how to tap into the power of those connections, they'll be left behind.

Show a Strong Hand

- Have you killed any collaboration projects in the past six months?
- Do you manage dynamically—forming and disbanding teams quickly as opportunities arise?
- Do the right people in your organization know they can "close" a discussion and make a decision?
- Does your team debate ideas vigorously but then unite behind decisions made?

Leaders today must be able to harness ideas, people, and resources from across boundaries of all kinds. That requires reinventing their talent strategies and building strong connections both inside and outside their organizations. To get all the disparate players to work together effectively, they also need to know when to wield influence rather than authority to move things forward, and when to halt unproductive discussions, squash politicking, and make final calls.

Differences in convictions, cultural values, and operating norms inevitably add complexity to collaborative efforts. But they also make them richer, more innovative, and more valuable. Getting that value is the heart of collaborative leadership.

Originally published in July–August 2011. Reprint R1107D

Social Intelligence and the Biology of Leadership

by Daniel Goleman and Richard Boyatzis

IN 1998, ONE OF US, Daniel Goleman, published in these pages his first article on emotional intelligence and leadership. The response to "What Makes a Leader?" was enthusiastic. People throughout and beyond the business community started talking about the vital role that empathy and self-knowledge play in effective leadership. The concept of emotional intelligence continues to occupy a prominent space in the leadership literature and in everyday coaching practices. But in the past five years, research in the emerging field of social neuroscience—the study of what happens in the brain while people interact—is beginning to reveal subtle new truths about what makes a good leader.

The salient discovery is that certain things leaders do—specifically, exhibit empathy and become attuned to others' moods—literally affect both their own brain chemistry and that of their followers. Indeed, researchers have found that the leader-follower dynamic is not a case of two (or more) independent brains reacting consciously or unconsciously to each other. Rather, the individual minds become, in a sense, fused into a single system. We believe that great leaders are those whose behavior powerfully leverages the system of brain interconnectedness. We place them on the opposite end of the neural continuum from people with serious social disorders, such as autism or Asperger's syndrome, that are characterized by underdevelopment in the areas of the brain associated with social interactions. If we are correct, it follows that a potent way of becoming a better leader is to find authentic contexts in which to learn the kinds of social behavior that reinforce the brain's social circuitry. Leading effectively is, in other words, less about mastering situations—or even mastering social skill sets—than about developing a genuine interest in and talent for fostering positive feelings in the people whose cooperation and support you need.

The notion that effective leadership is about having powerful social circuits in the brain has prompted us to extend our concept of emotional intelligence, which we had grounded in theories of individual psychology. A more relationship-based construct for assessing leadership is *social intelligence,* which we define as a set of interpersonal competencies built on specific neural circuits (and related endocrine systems) that inspire others to be effective.

The idea that leaders need social skills is not new, of course. In 1920, Columbia University psychologist Edward Thorndike pointed out that "the best mechanic in a factory may fail as a foreman for lack of social intelligence." More recently, our colleague Claudio Fernández-Aráoz found in an analysis of new C-level executives that those who had been hired for their self-discipline, drive, and intellect were sometimes later fired for lacking basic social skills. In other words, the people Fernández-Aráoz studied had smarts in spades, but their inability to get along socially on the job was professionally self-defeating.

What's new about our definition of social intelligence is its biological underpinning, which we will explore in the following pages. Drawing on the work of neuroscientists, our own research and consulting endeavors, and the findings of researchers affiliated with the Consortium for Research on Emotional Intelligence in Organizations, we will show you how to translate newly acquired knowledge about mirror neurons, spindle cells, and oscillators into practical, socially intelligent behaviors that can reinforce the neural links between you and your followers.

Idea in Brief

Your behavior can energize—or deflate—your entire organization through **mood contagion**. For example, if you laugh often and set an easygoing tone, you'll trigger similar behaviors among your team members. Shared behaviors unify a team, and bonded groups perform better than fragmented ones.

Mood contagion stems from neurobiology. Positive behaviors—such as exhibiting empathy—create a chemical connection between a leader's and his or her followers' brains. By managing those interconnections adroitly, leaders can deliver measurable business results. For example, after one executive at a *Fortune* 500 company worked with a coach and role model to improve her behavior, employee retention and emotional commitment in her unit soared. And the unit's annual sales jumped 6%.

How to foster the neurobiological changes that create positive behaviors and emotions in your employees? Goleman and Boyatzis advise sharpening your **social intelligence** skills.

Followers Mirror Their Leaders—Literally

Perhaps the most stunning recent discovery in behavioral neuroscience is the identification of *mirror neurons* in widely dispersed areas of the brain. Italian neuroscientists found them by accident while monitoring a particular cell in a monkey's brain that fired only when the monkey raised its arm. One day a lab assistant lifted an ice cream cone to his own mouth and triggered a reaction in the monkey's cell. It was the first evidence that the brain is peppered with neurons that mimic, or mirror, what another being does. This previously unknown class of brain cells operates as neural Wi-Fi, allowing us to navigate our social world. When we consciously or unconsciously detect someone else's emotions through their actions, our mirror neurons reproduce those emotions. Collectively, these neurons create an instant sense of shared experience.

Mirror neurons have particular importance in organizations, because leaders' emotions and actions prompt followers to mirror those feelings and deeds. The effects of activating neural circuitry in followers' brains can be very powerful. In a recent study, our

Idea in Practice

Identify Social Strengths and Weaknesses

Social intelligence skills include the following. Identify which ones you're good at—and which ones need improvement.

Skill	Do you . . .
Empathy	Understand what motivates other people, even those from different backgrounds? Are you sensitive to their needs?
Attunement	Listen attentively and think about how others feel? Are you attuned to others' moods?
Organizational Awareness	Appreciate your group's or organization's culture and values? Understand social networks and know their unspoken norms?
Influence	Persuade others by engaging them in discussion, appealing to their interests, and getting support from key people?
Developing Others	Coach and mentor others with compassion? Do you personally invest time and energy in mentoring and provide feedback that people find helpful for their professional development?
Inspiration	Articulate a compelling vision, build group pride, foster a positive emotional tone, and lead by bringing out the best in people?
Teamwork	Encourage the participation of everyone on your team, support all members, and foster cooperation?

colleague Marie Dasborough observed two groups: One received negative performance feedback accompanied by positive emotional signals—namely, nods and smiles; the other was given positive feedback that was delivered critically, with frowns and narrowed eyes. In subsequent interviews conducted to compare the emotional states of the two groups, the people who had received positive feedback accompanied by negative emotional signals reported feeling worse about their performance than did

Craft a Plan for Change

Now determine how you'll strengthen your social intelligence. Working with a coach—who can debrief you about what she observes—and learning directly from a role model are particularly powerful ways to make needed behavioral changes.

> *Example:* Janice was hired as a marketing manager for her business expertise, strategic thinking powers, and ability to deal with obstacles to crucial goals. But within her first six months on the job, she was floundering. Other executives saw her as aggressive and opinionated—as well as careless about what she said and to whom.

Her boss called in a coach, who administered a 360-degree evaluation. Findings revealed that Janice didn't know how to establish rapport with people, notice their reactions to her, read social norms, or recognize others' emotional cues when she violated those norms. Through coaching, Janice learned to express her ideas with conviction (instead of with pit bull–like determination) and to disagree with others without damaging relationships.

By switching to a job where she reported to a socially intelligent mentor, Janice further strengthened her skills, including learning how to critique others' performance in productive ways. She was promoted to a position two levels up where, with additional coaching, she mastered reading cues from direct reports who were still signaling frustration with her. Her company's investment in her (along with her own commitment to change) paid big dividends—in the form of lower turnover and higher sales in Janice's multibillion-dollar unit.

the participants who had received good-natured negative feedback. In effect, the delivery was more important than the message itself. And everybody knows that when people feel better, they perform better. So, if leaders hope to get the best out of their people, they should continue to be demanding but in ways that foster a positive mood in their teams. The old carrot-and-stick approach alone doesn't make neural sense; traditional incentive systems are simply not enough to get the best performance from followers.

Here's an example of what does work. It turns out that there's a subset of mirror neurons whose only job is to detect other people's smiles and laughter, prompting smiles and laughter in return. A boss who is self-controlled and humorless will rarely engage those neurons in his team members, but a boss who laughs and sets an easygoing tone puts those neurons to work, triggering spontaneous laughter and knitting his team together in the process. A bonded group is one that performs well, as our colleague Fabio Sala has shown in his research. He found that top-performing leaders elicited laughter from their subordinates three times as often, on average, as did midperforming leaders. Being in a good mood, other research finds, helps people take in information effectively and respond nimbly and creatively. In other words, laughter is serious business.

It certainly made a difference at one university-based hospital in Boston. Two doctors we'll call Dr. Burke and Dr. Humboldt were in contention for the post of CEO of the corporation that ran this hospital and others. Both of them headed up departments, were superb physicians, and had published many widely cited research articles in prestigious medical journals. But the two had very different personalities. Burke was intense, task focused, and impersonal. He was a relentless perfectionist with a combative tone that kept his staff continually on edge. Humboldt was no less demanding, but he was very approachable, even playful, in relating to staff, colleagues, and patients. Observers noted that people smiled and teased one another—and even spoke their minds—more in Humboldt's department than in Burke's. Prized talent often ended up leaving Burke's department; in contrast, outstanding folks gravitated to Humboldt's warmer working climate. Recognizing Humboldt's socially intelligent leadership style, the hospital corporation's board picked him as the new CEO.

The "Finely Attuned" Leader

Great executives often talk about leading from the gut. Indeed, having good instincts is widely recognized as an advantage for a leader in any context, whether in reading the mood of one's organization or in conducting a delicate negotiation with the competition. Leadership scholars characterize this talent as an ability to recognize patterns, usually born of extensive experience. Their advice: Trust your gut, but get lots of input as you make decisions. That's sound practice, of course, but managers don't always have the time to consult dozens of people.

Findings in neuroscience suggest that this approach is probably too cautious. Intuition, too, is in the brain, produced in part by a class of neurons called *spindle cells* because of their shape. They have a body size about four times that of other brain cells, with an extra-long branch to make attaching to other cells easier and transmitting thoughts and feelings to them quicker. This ultrarapid connection of emotions, beliefs, and judgments creates what behavioral scientists call our social guidance system. Spindle cells trigger neural networks that come into play whenever we have to choose the best response among many—even for a task as routine as prioritizing a to-do list. These cells also help us gauge whether someone is trustworthy and right (or wrong) for a job. Within one-twentieth of a second, our spindle cells fire with information about how we feel about that person; such "thin-slice" judgments can be very accurate, as follow-up metrics reveal. Therefore, leaders should not fear to act on those judgments, provided that they are also attuned to others' moods.

Such attunement is literally physical. Followers of an effective leader experience rapport with her—or what we and our colleague Annie McKee call "resonance." Much of this feeling arises unconsciously, thanks to mirror neurons and spindle-cell circuitry. But another class of neurons is also involved: *Oscillators* coordinate people physically by regulating how and when their bodies move together. You can see oscillators in action when you watch people about to kiss; their movements look like a dance, one body responding to the other seamlessly. The same dynamic occurs when two cellists play together. Not only do they hit their notes in unison, but thanks to oscillators, the two musicians' right brain hemispheres are more closely coordinated than are the left and right sides of their individual brains.

Do Women Have Stronger Social Circuits?

PEOPLE OFTEN ASK WHETHER GENDER differences factor into the social intelligence skills needed for outstanding leadership. The answer is yes and no. It's true that women tend, on average, to be better than men at immediately sensing other people's emotions, whereas men tend to have more social confidence, at least in work settings. However, gender differences in social intelligence that are dramatic in the general population are all but absent among the most successful leaders.

When the University of Toledo's Margaret Hopkins studied several hundred executives from a major bank, she found gender differences in social intelligence in the overall group but not between the most effective men and the most effective women. Ruth Malloy of the Hay Group uncovered a similar pattern in her study of CEOs of international companies. Gender, clearly, is not neural destiny.

Firing Up Your Social Neurons

The firing of social neurons is evident all around us. We once analyzed a video of Herb Kelleher, a cofounder and former CEO of Southwest Airlines, strolling down the corridors of Love Field in Dallas, the airline's hub. We could practically see him activate the mirror neurons, oscillators, and other social circuitry in each person he encountered. He offered beaming smiles, shook hands with customers as he told them how much he appreciated their business, hugged employees as he thanked them for their good work. And he got back exactly what he gave. Typical was the flight attendant whose face lit up when she unexpectedly encountered her boss. "Oh, my honey!" she blurted, brimming with warmth, and gave him a big hug. She later explained, "Everyone just feels like family with him."

Unfortunately, it's not easy to turn yourself into a Herb Kelleher or a Dr. Humboldt if you're not one already. We know of no clear-cut methods to strengthen mirror neurons, spindle cells, and oscillators; they activate by the thousands per second during any encounter, and their precise firing patterns remain elusive. What's more, self-conscious attempts to display social intelligence can often backfire. When you make an intentional effort to coordinate movements with another person, it is not only oscillators that fire. In such situations the brain uses other, less adept circuitry to initiate and guide movements; as a result, the interaction feels forced.

The only way to develop your social circuitry effectively is to undertake the hard work of changing your behavior (see "Primal Leadership: The Hidden Driver of Great Performance," our December 2001 HBR article with Annie McKee). Companies interested in leadership development need to begin by assessing the willingness of individuals to enter a change program. Eager candidates should first develop a personal vision for change and then undergo a thorough diagnostic assessment, akin to a medical workup, to identify areas of social weakness and strength. Armed with the feedback, the aspiring leader can be trained in specific areas where developing better social skills will have the greatest payoff. The training can range from rehearsing better ways of interacting and trying them out at every opportunity, to being shadowed by a coach and then debriefed about what he observes, to learning directly from a role model. The options are many, but the road to success is always tough.

How to Become Socially Smarter

To see what social intelligence training involves, consider the case of a top executive we'll call Janice. She had been hired as a marketing manager by a *Fortune* 500 company because of her business expertise, outstanding track record as a strategic thinker and planner, reputation as a straight talker, and ability to anticipate business issues that were crucial for meeting goals. Within her first six months on the job, however, Janice was floundering; other executives saw her as aggressive and opinionated, lacking in political astuteness, and careless about what she said and to whom, especially higher-ups.

To save this promising leader, Janice's boss called in Kathleen Cavallo, an organizational psychologist and senior consultant with the Hay Group, who immediately put Janice through a 360-degree evaluation. Her direct reports, peers, and managers gave Janice low ratings on empathy, service orientation, adaptability, and managing conflicts. Cavallo learned more by having confidential conversations with the people who worked most closely with Janice. Their complaints focused on her failure to establish rapport with people or even notice their reactions. The bottom line: Janice was adept neither at reading the social norms of a group nor at recognizing people's emotional cues when she violated those norms. Even more dangerous, Janice did not realize she was being too blunt in managing upward. When she had a strong difference of opinion with a manager, she did not sense when to back off. Her "let's get it all on the table and mix it up" approach was threatening her job; top management was getting fed up.

When Cavallo presented this performance feedback as a wake-up call to Janice, she was of course shaken to discover that her job might be in danger. What upset her more, though, was the realization that she was not having her desired impact on other people. Cavallo initiated coaching sessions in which Janice would describe notable successes and failures from her day. The more time Janice spent reviewing these incidents, the better she became at recognizing the difference between expressing an idea with conviction and acting like a pit bull. She began to anticipate how people might react to her in a meeting or during a negative performance review; she rehearsed more-astute ways to present her opinions; and she developed a personal vision for change. Such mental preparation activates the social circuitry of the brain, strengthening the neural connections you need to act effectively; that's why Olympic athletes put hundreds of hours into mental review of their moves.

At one point, Cavallo asked Janice to name a leader in her organization who had excellent social intelligence skills. Janice identified a veteran senior manager who was masterly both in the art of the critique and at expressing disagreement in meetings without damaging relationships. She asked him to help coach her, and she switched to a job where she could work with him—a post she held for two years. Janice was lucky to find a mentor who believed that part of a leader's job is to develop human capital. Many bosses would rather manage around a problem employee than help her get better. Janice's new boss took her on because he recognized her other strengths as invaluable, and his gut told him that Janice could improve with guidance.

Before meetings, Janice's mentor coached her on how to express her viewpoint about contentious issues and how to talk to higher-ups, and he modeled for her the art of performance feedback. By observing him day in and day out, Janice learned to affirm people even as she challenged their positions or critiqued their performance. Spending time with a living, breathing model of effective behavior provides the perfect stimulation for our mirror neurons, which allow us to directly experience, internalize, and ultimately emulate what we observe.

Janice's transformation was genuine and comprehensive. In a sense, she went in one person and came out another. If you think about it, that's an important lesson from neuroscience: Because our behavior creates and develops neural networks, we are not necessarily prisoners of our genes and our early childhood experiences. Leaders can change if, like Janice, they are ready to put in the effort. As she progressed in her training, the social behaviors she was learning became more like second nature to her. In scientific terms, Janice was strengthening her social circuits through practice. And as others responded to her, their brains connected with hers more profoundly and effectively, thereby reinforcing Janice's circuits in a virtuous circle. The upshot: Janice went from being on the verge of dismissal to getting promoted to a position two levels up.

A few years later, some members of Janice's staff left the company because they were not happy—so she asked Cavallo to come back. Cavallo discovered that although Janice had mastered the ability to communicate and connect with management and peers, she still sometimes missed cues from her direct reports when they tried to signal their frustration. With more help from Cavallo, Janice was able to turn the situation around by refocusing her attention on her staff's emotional needs and fine-tuning her communication style. Opinion surveys conducted with Janice's staff before and after Cavallo's second round of coaching documented dramatic increases in their emotional commitment and intention to stay in the organization. Janice and the staff also delivered a 6% increase in annual sales, and after another successful year she was made president of a

Are You a Socially Intelligent Leader?

TO MEASURE AN EXECUTIVE'S SOCIAL intelligence and help him or her develop a plan for improving it, we have a specialist administer our behavioral assessment tool, the Emotional and Social Competency Inventory. It is a 360-degree evaluation instrument by which bosses, peers, direct reports, clients, and sometimes even family members assess a leader according to seven social intelligence qualities.

We came up with these seven by integrating our existing emotional intelligence framework with data assembled by our colleagues at the Hay Group, who used hard metrics to capture the behavior of top-performing leaders at hundreds of corporations over two decades. Listed here are each of the qualities, followed by some of the questions we use to assess them.

Empathy

- Do you understand what motivates other people, even those from different backgrounds?
- Are you sensitive to others' needs?

Attunement

- Do you listen attentively and think about how others feel?
- Are you attuned to others' moods?

Organizational Awareness

- Do you appreciate the culture and values of the group or organization?
- Do you understand social networks and know their unspoken norms?

multibillion-dollar unit. Companies can clearly benefit a lot from putting people through the kind of program Janice completed.

Hard Metrics of Social Intelligence

Our research over the past decade has confirmed that there is a large performance gap between socially intelligent and socially unintelligent leaders. At a major national bank, for example, we found that levels of an executive's social intelligence competencies predicted yearly performance appraisals more powerfully than did the emotional intelligence competencies of self-awareness and

Influence

- Do you persuade others by engaging them in discussion and appealing to their self-interests?
- Do you get support from key people?

Developing Others

- Do you coach and mentor others with compassion and personally invest time and energy in mentoring?
- Do you provide feedback that people find helpful for their professional development?

Inspiration

- Do you articulate a compelling vision, build group pride, and foster a positive emotional tone?
- Do you lead by bringing out the best in people?

Teamwork

- Do you solicit input from everyone on the team?
- Do you support all team members and encourage cooperation?

self-management. (For a brief explanation of our assessment tool, which focuses on seven dimensions, see the sidebar "Are You a Socially Intelligent Leader?")

Social intelligence turns out to be especially important in crisis situations. Consider the experience of workers at a large Canadian provincial health care system that had gone through drastic cutbacks and a reorganization. Internal surveys revealed that the frontline workers had become frustrated that they were no longer able to give their patients a high level of care. Notably, workers whose leaders scored low in social intelligence reported unmet patient-care needs at three times the rate—and emotional exhaustion at four times the

The Chemistry of Stress

WHEN PEOPLE ARE UNDER STRESS, surges in the stress hormones adrenaline and cortisol strongly affect their reasoning and cognition. At low levels, cortisol facilitates thinking and other mental functions, so well-timed pressure to perform and targeted critiques of subordinates certainly have their place. When a leader's demands become too great for a subordinate to handle, however, soaring cortisol levels and an added hard kick of adrenaline can paralyze the mind's critical abilities. Attention fixates on the threat from the boss rather than the work at hand; memory, planning, and creativity go out the window. People fall back on old habits, no matter how unsuitable those are for addressing new challenges.

Poorly delivered criticism and displays of anger by leaders are common triggers of hormonal surges. In fact, when laboratory scientists want to study the highest levels of stress hormones, they simulate a job interview in which an applicant receives intense face-to-face criticism—an analogue of a boss's tearing apart a subordinate's performance. Researchers likewise find that when someone who is very important to a person expresses contempt or disgust toward him, his stress circuitry triggers an explosion by stress hormones and a spike in heart rate of 30 to 40 beats per minute. Then, because of the interpersonal dynamic of mirror neurons and oscillators, the tension spreads to other people. Before you know it, the destructive emotions have infected an entire group and inhibited its performance.

Leaders are themselves not immune to the contagion of stress. All the more reason they should take the time to understand the biology of their emotions.

---

rate—of their colleagues who had supportive leaders. At the same time, nurses with socially intelligent bosses reported good emotional health and an enhanced ability to care for their patients, even during the stress of layoffs (see the sidebar "The Chemistry of Stress"). These results should be compulsory reading for the boards of companies in crisis. Such boards typically favor expertise over social intelligence when selecting someone to guide the institution through tough times. A crisis manager needs both.

As we explore the discoveries of neuroscience, we are struck by how closely the best psychological theories of development map to the newly charted hardwiring of the brain. Back in the 1950s, for example, British pediatrician and psychoanalyst D.W. Winnicott was advocating for play as a way to accelerate children's learning. Similarly, British physician and psychoanalyst John Bowlby emphasized the importance of providing a secure base from which people can strive toward goals, take risks without unwarranted fear, and freely explore new possibilities. Hard-bitten executives may consider it absurdly indulgent and financially untenable to concern themselves with such theories in a world where bottom-line performance is the yardstick of success. But as new ways of scientifically measuring human development start to bear out these theories and link them directly with performance, the so-called soft side of business begins to look not so soft after all.

Originally published in September 2008. Reprint R0809E

Bringing Minds Together

by John Abele

WHEN I WAS invited to submit an article to this spotlight on collaboration, the first question I asked was whether the other contributors and I would have the chance to interact and perhaps integrate our ideas on the topic. I knew that *Harvard Business Review* was deeply rooted in a scholarly tradition—and that worried me. Academic collaboration, I've learned over the years, is something of an oxymoron. More often than not, what is described by that term is really noncollaborative, or worse, pseudo-collaborative work, driven by the long-standing rituals of institutional seniority and the professional and financial incentives to build higher silos with thicker walls. That's a shame since it is our universities that are supposed to have the intellectual force and license to find bold solutions to important problems. On the bright side, there's an extraordinary opportunity for those of us nonacademics who, unconstrained by those customs, see value in getting silos to collide.

The individuals in the stories you are about to read were naturally skillful silo-colliders. Their success in breaking down barriers between and within the scientific, medical, academic, and business communities taught me most of what I know about making progress through collaboration.

My perspective is that of an entrepreneur whose entire career has involved breakthrough innovations, mostly in the scientific and

Community Building

begins with convincing people who don't need to work together that they should. This depends on:

- Inspiring them with a vision of change that is beyond any of their powers to bring about individually

- Convincing them that the other collaborators are vital to the effort and equal to the challenge

- Preventing any one party from benefiting so much that the others feel their contributions are being exploited

medical domains. This wasn't "serial entrepreneurship"—it was long-slog enterprise building in an environment where much of what my colleagues and I did was viewed as politically incorrect. We were developing new approaches that had huge potential value for customers and society but required that well-trained practitioners change their behavior. Despite the clear logic behind the products we invented, markets for them didn't exist. We had to create them in the face of considerable resistance from players invested in the old way and threatened with a loss of power, prestige, and money. Prospects had to be sold on not just our solution but our reframing of the problem, requiring from them a lot of learning—and unlearning of old techniques. Any of the products could have served as the poster child for what Clay Christensen calls "disruptive innovation."

Cash Up Front and Build It Yourself

I got my first glimpse of that kind of collaboration many decades ago, but it continues to teach me lessons to this day. Shortly after I graduated from college (Amherst '59), I went to work for a small company in the Boston area called Advanced Instruments. The lab instruments it made—an osmometer that measured particle concentrations in solutions and a flame photometer that measured ions in solutions—were new to the marketplace, so we regularly invested in booths at the major conferences and trade shows. When traffic in the booth was slow, we'd spend time getting to know folks from

Idea in Brief

Boston Scientific founder John Abele has been party to his share of groundbreaking innovations over the years. But the revolutionary advances in medical science that these breakthroughs brought about were not the efforts of one firm alone, let alone one inventor.

Abele tells two fascinating stories of collaboration—one about Jack Whitehead's upending of hospitals' blood and urine testing procedures and the other about Andreas Gruentzig's success in bringing balloon catheterization into the cardiology mainstream. Both Whitehead and Gruentzig spearheaded the emergence of entirely new fields, bringing together scientist-customers to voluntarily develop standards, training programs, new business models, and even a specialized language to describe their new field.

The process of collaboration, Abele says, is fraught with contradictions and subtlety. It takes consummate leadership skills to persuade others to spend countless hours solving important problems in partnership with people they don't necessarily like. Moreover, managing egos so that each person's commitment, energy, and creativity is unleashed in a way that doesn't disadvantage others requires an impresario personality. Finally, true authenticity—something that few people can project—is critical for earning customers' trust and convincing them that their valuable contributions won't be used for anything other than moving the technology forward.

neighboring exhibits. At one of those conferences, in 1960, I met Jack Whitehead, the CEO of Technicon. I subsequently came to know his company pretty well. Its success is more than just a surprising business story. It's the kind of effort Margaret Mead had in mind when she said, "Never underestimate the power of a small dedicated group of people to change the world. Indeed, it's the only thing that ever has."

Technicon was originally a maker of tissue-processing equipment, and that was a nice business, but slow growing. Jack had been on the lookout for new technologies that would allow him to dramatically expand his business. He made the bold decision to buy the patents and prototypes for a machine that automated the process of analyzing certain chemicals. The doctor who'd invented the machine was a clinical chemist—the person who runs the hospital lab that tests blood, urine, and other body fluids—and his creation was truly amazing. The liquid samples poured into it were transported through transparent tubing made of hydrophobic (water-repelling) materials. Each sample beaded up in the tube rather than spreading out. Air bubbles separated the samples and prevented cross-contamination. Along their journey through the "bubble machine," the samples would pass through a spectrometer, a device that determines the absorption of various wavelengths of light in a liquid sample and thereby indicates what chemicals, and in what quantities, are present.

The inventor was, naturally, proud of his achievement. But when he tried to sell it to the big laboratory supply companies of the time, he was turned down flat. That may seem baffling, given the fact that such instruments now constitute a multibillion-dollar business, with millions of tests being carried out daily. But this was the early 1960s, when physicians were ordering very few tests, and there were plenty of lab technicians to do them. Even the leading instrument makers couldn't see the point of automating the process. More important, the professional societies weren't on board. Not only did they believe that no more tests were needed, they were downright hostile to any outsider who had the temerity to tell them otherwise. To say that this was a new and disruptive technology without a defined market would be an understatement. And although the big companies were pretty good at selling accepted products, they were not (and still are not) up to that kind of challenge. Even if they could envision the change such a machine would usher in, they couldn't manage the culture-changing activities that go with creating new markets. But Jack could.

His outgoing personality and powers of persuasion worked in his favor, but he also came up with a radical sales process. Pointing out that the instrument was new and would remain unique because it was protected by lots of patents, he told all interested buyers that they'd have to spend a week at his factory learning about it—and that payment was required in advance. The training would cover how the instrument worked, what might go wrong, how to fix it, how to use it for different applications, and how to develop new applications. Customers even had to put their own machines together.

Those might sound like terms that would discourage people from buying the machine. A week is a long time for busy scientists, and the factory was nothing fancy. Demanding the money up front seemed pretty aggressive. But every field has its early adopters, and Jack was good at finding them.

The real magic of the approach, however, was in the extraordinary dynamic it created among the participants. Working in Technicon's factory, thinking about applications, they didn't feel like customers, they felt like partners. They got to know Jack and his staff. They worked like the devil during the day and played pretty hard at night—sometimes the reverse. They got to know one another very well. They became a kind of family.

When the week ended, those relationships endured and a vibrant community began to emerge around the innovation. The scientist-customers fixed one another's machines. They developed new applications. They published papers. They came up with new product ideas. They gave talks at scientific meetings. They recruited new customers. In time, they developed standards, training programs, new business models, and even a specialized language to describe their new field.

It wasn't long before Jack's "band of brothers" had become sufficiently large and was producing so many new ideas that he decided to convene what he called the Technicon Symposium. This was pretty heretical since academic societies planned and sponsored all the scientific conferences at the time; companies like Technicon were relegated to the exhibit halls. But the symposium served a clear need, and over the years it grew in size and prestige until it rivaled the professional societies' meetings in quality and reputation. Jack had formed a "user group" long before that strategy had been conceived. He had created a culture in which everyone was both a leader and a follower. It wasn't about money; it was about being a pioneer in a new field.

Watching how this unique strategy helped the field advance and Technicon succeed had a profound effect on me. Most of my colleagues saw what Jack was doing as creative marketing and aggressive business strategy. But I saw it differently, and by now I know that something much bigger was actually going on. He was launching a new field that could be created only by collaboration—and collaboration among people who had previously seen no need to work together. Thanks to Jack's efforts, a group of scientist-customers self-organized to do something he never could have done on his own: advance the responsible development of automated chemical analysis.

As I watched this experiment evolve, and later applied its lessons in my work and philanthropic activities, I came to realize that the kind of collaboration Jack made look simple is in fact a process fraught with contradictions and subtlety. It takes a great collaborative leader. Persuading people to contribute countless hours of effort in partnership with people they don't necessarily like to solve important problems requires consummate leadership skills. Managing egos so that each person's commitment, energy, and creativity is unleashed in a way without disadvantaging others demands an impresario personality. Earning customers' trust and convincing them that their valuable contributions won't be used for anything other than moving the technology forward requires an authenticity few people can project.

The interaction and progress Jack enabled was never heralded as collaboration, though that is what it was. Indeed, I've learned that some of the best collaborative efforts don't look like collaborations. And some projects that are touted as collaborations are Potemkin villages—great-looking facades with no substance behind them.

Two Inventors, One Breakthrough

In 1967 I left Advanced Instruments on friendly terms. Having risen from a sales engineer to general manager of that privately owned company, I was eager to strike out on my own. I soon bought a fledgling start-up called Medi-Tech, which later became Boston Scientific. Its product was a steerable catheter—an amazing integration of chemical, polymeric, metallurgical, mechanical, and processing technologies that allowed users (practitioners in radiology, cardiology, gastroenterology, and urology) to use fluoroscopic imaging to remotely guide a catheter or device to any location in the body. To advance the technology and build a market for it, I turned to Jack Whitehead's strategy of creating a community of users to share applications, education, and research. Although the field wasn't that big, our technology was visibly impressive to brilliant inventor-physicians, and our collaborative strategy differentiated us. We lacked the resources and name recognition that many of our competitors had, but we became known as trustworthy innovators who would listen, share, and ask good questions. Our competitors vied to take opinion leaders out to dinner. Opinion leaders took us out.

Our collaborative outreach led us to a young angiologist by the name of Andreas Gruentzig, who had developed a balloon catheter (a tube with a sausage-shaped balloon at the tip) for the purpose of enlarging narrowed arteries without surgery. He actually built the devices in the kitchen of his apartment, using a razor, tubing, and adhesive.

The basic idea of opening arteries with a catheter, called percutaneous transluminal angioplasty, had been pioneered a decade earlier by a doctor from Oregon, Charles Dotter. But Dotter's technique never took off. Why? In the first place, he used a tapered catheter that simply "snowplowed" the obstructing material to the side or sometimes just pushed it downstream. Gruentzig's balloon was much less traumatic and more effective. Just as important, Dotter's stance toward his potential community pretty much ensured that he would not get the feedback he needed to improve the technology. A classic inventor, he was an exciting speaker but tended to exaggerate claims. He also loved telling surgeons that they'd be out of business in the near future—not a good strategy if he hoped for their help.

Andreas was just as passionate about his ideas, and a magnetic speaker in his own way, but he was understated, careful, and curious. He was an inventor, a technician, an excellent clinician who connected with patients, and a good experimentalist who knew how to design a well-thought-out trial. I should also note that, as a junior

Establishment Bucking

can't be avoided. When a group collaborates on a new solution, there's usually another, bigger, group invested in the way things are done today. Be sure to:

- Recruit some of their respected players into your vanguard
- Create your own center stage to prevent your star project from being pushed into the wings
- Downplay, rather than underscore, the threat your breakthrough poses to their livelihood

---

physician at the University Hospital in Zurich, he had very little personal or professional authority. Much of his early access and influence was thanks to his friendship with a world-famous cardiac surgeon named Ake Senning, the father of the pacemaker, who had moved from Sweden to Switzerland for tax reasons. Senning's patronage was the reason that Andreas had patients on which to try his new procedure. (Of course, Andreas didn't start with patients; he spent years practicing in the lab on dogs and then cadavers before taking on low-risk patients who could be easily moved to surgery if the procedure was unsuccessful.)

Andreas turned out to be an extraordinary collaborative leader. He presented his ideas in ways that cried out for input from other brilliant minds. Instead of proclaiming that his ideas were revolutionary breakthroughs that would change medicine, Andreas referred to them as incremental advances. He was always the first to point out the deficiencies in the tools he pioneered and was constantly on the lookout for signs that they were flawed. He sought ideas from anyone who might be able to help address problems. He won over surgeons—the very people whose work he was disrupting and thus who were his potential enemies—by presenting all his data in an understated way. People responded in part because of Andreas's unusual willingness to share credit for whatever was achieved. He used the word "we," not "I," when describing the efforts that had made the breakthroughs possible.

Collaboration

is the natural by-product of leaders who are

- Passionately curious—who crave new insights and suspect that others have them

- Modestly confident—who can bounce ideas off brilliant collaborators, without turning it into a competition

- Mildly obsessed—who care more about the collective mission than about how achieving it will benefit their personal fortunes

. . . and may be the only leadership mode that produces breakthrough results.

A Course Becomes a Cause

In the fall of 1976, Andreas presented a poster on his animal work at the American Heart Association's annual meeting, advancing the powerful but controversial idea that balloon catheterization could be used to open coronary arteries. I introduced many of my cardiology and surgeon friends to him at the meeting. Their conversations were so compelling that a number of physicians made plans right then to fly to Switzerland and see firsthand what he was doing. In fact, so many people visited him or invited him to their institutions to demonstrate his procedure that his boss in Zurich put a moratorium on visits and trips.

Undeterred, Andreas found a way around the restrictions. He created a course that would bring all the parties together. He used the then-new capabilities of video to transmit images from the cath lab where he would conduct the procedure to a lecture theatre at the hospital. His innovative approach was a smashing success. It allowed him to share with the audience every detail of how the technology worked, including any problems that arose. To make sure that everyone was engaged, he would periodically ask participants, via video, what they thought he should do next. That willingness to take direction communicated his belief that he and his scientist-customers were equals and this wasn't his project alone. On the last evening of the course, dinner was served on a local hilltop, and a bonfire and torches provided light as the sun went down. At the end of the evening Andreas led his guests in a torchlight parade down the hill. The symbolism was powerful: Everyone was royalty. This group was going to change the world.

What Andreas couldn't have known in that first year was how his idea of a live demonstration course would evolve. Other physicians started their own live demonstration courses on the same principles. When audiences became too large for hospital lecture halls, they began meeting in hotel ballrooms and in convention centers. A moderated panel of contrarian, independent experts would provide play-by-play critical analysis for everyone's benefit. Outside speakers were invited to present slide talks during the downtime between cases. The leading physician educators used audience-response technology to engage participants on difficult issues.

Most strikingly, it proved to be only a short hop hosting on-site meetings to conducting off-site and offshore ones. For example, American medical specialists were eager to learn about technologies not yet approved by the FDA, and the performance and price of video technology made it feasible to view live coverage of cases being performed in other countries. Some courses today assemble many thousands of physicians and involve more than 100 different live cases beamed in from cities around the world.

At that scale, the live demonstration course tends to be thought of as a learning experience, pure and simple, but I would describe it as one of those collaborations that doesn't look like one. All sides of issues and a wide range of perspectives are presented, and controversy is welcomed. As in Andreas's first course, the goal is a collective one: to advance the field through the sharing of research, best practices, trial status, clinical status, and what's coming next.

Creating the Basis for Progress

Perhaps the most important collaborative approach Andreas introduced was the creation of a voluntary registry of the cases he and a few of his U.S. colleagues treated. In contrast to the stultifying record keeping required by "official" bureaucratic entities, this was a way to track results independent of any traditional professional society or academic or government institution. At that time, the FDA had the authority to regulate medical devices, but it was a long way away from figuring out the process details for doing so. That first registry was conceived to generate a body of data that could help the community understand which factors were the most important for success, what needed to be improved, and how the instruments might be modified to safely treat more types of blockages. Cardiologists doing these procedures were pressured by peers to produce careful documentation. Perhaps, as a result, most were a bit less likely to behave recklessly. It is no exaggeration to say that the rapid sharing of experience and techniques enabled by the registry saved many lives and prevented untold complications. There was no long wait, as in a drug trial, for lessons to be extracted; clinical users could take advantage of new information as soon as it came in. Problems were discovered and solutions were offered almost on the fly. And when it came time to publish papers, Andreas and his closest collaborators made sure to spread the intellectual wealth. They developed guidelines for which papers would be published by which authors and when.

By the time the registry was picked up by the National Institutes of Health, several years later, it was well-established as a powerful new methodology in itself. This was the first time that so many physicians had collaborated on a new technique, and it was clear that the collaboration had accelerated both the development of the technique and the learning about it. The approach has since been adopted in many other fields.

A Different Kind of Leadership

One thing that has become clear in the course of this proliferation of registries is how dependent they turn out to be on the capabilities of their leaders. The ability to lead leaders is a rare skill, and Andreas, like Jack Whitehead, was a great role model. In a sense, he was the Linus Torvalds or Jimmy Wales of angioplasty. Just as Torvalds helped spawn the open source movement, and Jimmy Wales spearheaded the Wiki phenomenon, Andreas had created a community of change agents who carried his ideas forward far more efficiently than he could have done on his own.

The key was the dynamic between Andreas and his followers. This was a group of big personalities, full of independent, ego-driven, enormously self-confident men. On top of that, they were rivals. But all of them loved working at the cutting edge of medicine and had dreamed of taking part in a groundbreaking endeavor. When Andreas came along, they saw that possibility. And that's one of the crucial ingredients of collaboration. None of the participants would have said Andreas had the right to give them orders, yet they respected him and were confident he was taking the right steps to ensure that the technology was properly assessed as it was developed. He had earned that confidence, paradoxically, by never presuming to have all the answers. He carefully explained why he did things the way he did, but he always allowed that others might choose alternative methods. Just as Jack Whitehead did with his early band of brothers, Andreas built a corps that prided itself on boldly taking the risks and doing the hard work needed to turn a compelling vision into reality.

With that dynamic established, Andreas didn't need to exert much authority. In fact, he purposely ceded control and applied himself to keeping trust levels high. He role-modeled the investigational discipline that would allay doubts about the process. And he expertly managed the various personalities in the group to keep jealousies or interpersonal friction to a minimum. He encouraged members to continually question and teach one another. He made sure that problems were rooted out, not glossed over, the more quickly to arrive at solutions.

Is It the Tools?

Mention the word "collaboration" to businesspeople today and they immediately think you're going to talk about software. The tech world is boiling over with new tools that enable groups large and small to instantly and easily share complex information and that facilitate and track contributions from many participants. But true collaboration requires more than handy applications—in fact, the same tools can just as easily derail or outright destroy collaboration. The availability of so much software doesn't so much solve our need for collaboration as heighten the difficulty of managing it. To make matters worse, rules and laws that inhibit collaboration continue to shift and clash. The world becomes bumpier in some ways as it becomes flatter in others. In the science domain, the information explosion has led to more silos, not fewer.

For all these reasons, it's more critical than ever to understand the complex soft elements, such as emotional intelligence, that are the makings of a strong collaborative culture. Many people go through the motions, but few know how to really collaborate. I am often struck by the behaviors of otherwise bright people who poison potentially rich collaborations, seemingly without realizing it.

———

Jack Whitehead and Andreas Gruentzig were true collaborative leaders. There have been people like them in every field throughout history. It may be an exaggeration to compare Jack and Andreas with Gandhi, Mandela, or Martin Luther King, Jr., but let's list the challenges they all faced: Silos with different cultures. Strong egos, messenger killers, and pontificators. Hidden agendas, cynicism, and groupthink. Diverse levels of understanding and a whole range of biases. All these factors make it hard to harness the collective intelligence of great (or even not so great) minds. These leaders overcame the obstacles.

You can be sure that Jack and Andreas didn't get it all right. They had their catastrophes along the way. But their default mind-set was inclusive and questioning, confident and humble. Both had a great sense of theater and used it effectively. They knew how to set the stage for collaboration and employ ritual, symbolism, or humor to disarm and inspire. They recognized that diversity is an antidote to groupthink.

When will these approaches start catching on in boardrooms, mayors' offices, and universities? Look around you. I think you'll see that they already are.

Originally published in July–August 2011. Reprint R1107F

Building a Collaborative Enterprise

by Paul Adler, Charles Heckscher,
and Laurence Prusak

A SOFTWARE ENGINEER we'll call James vividly remembers his first day at Computer Sciences Corporation (CSC). The very first message he received: "Here are your Instructions" (yes, with a capital I).

"I thought I was bringing the know-how I'd need to do my job," James recalls. "But sure enough, you open up the Instructions, and it tells you how to do your job: how to lay the code out, where on the form to write a change-request number, and so on. I was shocked."

In this division at CSC, code is no longer developed by individual, freewheeling programmers. They now follow the Capability Maturity Model (CMM), a highly organized process that James initially felt was too bureaucratic: "As a developer, I was pretty allergic to all this paperwork. It's so time-consuming."

Not anymore. "I can see the need for it now," James says. "Now I'm just one of 30 or 40 people who may have to work on this code, so we need a change-request number that everyone can use to identify it. I can see that it makes things much easier."

What James was joining at CSC was neither a code-writing assembly line nor a bunch of autonomous hackers but a new type of organization that excels at combining the knowledge of diverse specialists. We call this kind of enterprise a *collaborative community.*

Collaborative communities encourage people to continually apply their unique talents to group projects—and to become motivated by a collective mission, not just personal gain or the intrinsic pleasures of autonomous creativity. By marrying a sense of common purpose to a supportive structure, these organizations are mobilizing knowledge workers' talents and expertise in flexible, highly manageable group-work efforts. The approach fosters not only innovation and agility but also efficiency and scalability.

A growing number of organizations—including IBM, Citibank, NASA, and Kaiser Permanente—are reaping the rewards of collaborative communities in the form of higher margins on knowledge-intensive work. (The CSC divisions that applied the CMM most rigorously reduced error rates by 75% over six years and achieved a 10% annual increase in productivity, while making products more innovative and technologically sophisticated.) We have found that such clear success requires four new organizational efforts:

- defining and building a shared purpose

- cultivating an ethic of contribution

- developing processes that enable people to work together in flexible but disciplined projects

- creating an infrastructure in which collaboration is valued and rewarded.

Our findings are based on many years of studying institutions that have sustained records of both efficiency and innovation. The writings of great thinkers in sociology—Karl Marx, Max Weber, Émile Durkheim, and Talcott Parsons—also inform our work. These classic figures were trying to make sense of broad economic and social changes during times when capitalism was mutating from small-scale manufacturing to large-scale industry. Our era represents just as momentous a shift, as we make the transition to an economy based on knowledge work and workers.

Idea in Brief

Can large companies be both innovative and efficient? Yes, argue Adler, of the University of Southern California; Heckscher, of Rutgers; and Prusak, an independent consultant. But they must develop new organizational capabilities that will create the atmosphere of trust that knowledge work requires—and the coordinating mechanisms to make it scalable. Specifically, such organizations must learn to:

- Define a shared purpose that guides what people at all levels of the organization are trying to achieve together;

- Cultivate an ethic of contribution in which the highest value is accorded to people who look beyond their specific roles and advance the common purpose;

- Develop scalable procedures for coordinating people's efforts so that process-management activities become truly interdependent; and

- Create an infrastructure in which individuals' spheres of influence overlap and collaboration is both valued and rewarded.

These four goals may sound idealized, but the imperative to achieve them is practical, say the authors. Only the truly collaborative enterprises that can tap into everyone's ideas—in an organized way—will compete imaginatively, quickly, and cost-effectively enough to become the household names of this century.

A Shared Purpose

Sociologist Max Weber famously outlined four bases for social relations, which can be roughly summarized as *tradition, self-interest, affection,* and *shared purpose.* Self-interest underlies what all businesses do, of course. The great industrial corporations of the 20th century also invoked tradition to motivate people. And many of the most innovative companies of the past 30 years—Hewlett-Packard, Microsoft, Apple, Google, and Facebook—have derived strength from strong, broadly felt affection for a charismatic leader.

In focusing on the fourth alternative—a shared purpose—collaborative communities seek a basis for trust and organizational cohesion that is more robust than self-interest, more flexible than tradition, and less ephemeral than the emotional, charismatic appeal of a Steve Jobs, a Larry Page, or a Mark Zuckerberg.

Like a good strategy or vision statement, an effective shared purpose articulates how a group will position itself in relation to competitors and partners—and what key contributions to customers and society will define its success. Kaiser Permanente's Value Compass, for example, succinctly defines the organization's shared purpose this way: "Best quality, best service, most affordable, best place to work."

This shared purpose is not an expression of a company's enduring essence—it's a description of what everyone in the organization is trying to do. It guides efforts at all levels of Kaiser: from top management's business strategy, to joint planning by the company's unique labor-management partnership, right down to unit-based teams' work on process improvement. In that regard, Value Compass is less a vision than a recognition of the challenges that every member of the group has the responsibility to meet every day. (See the sidebar "A Collaborative Dance at Kaiser Permanente.")

Leaders often have trouble articulating such a purpose, falling back on either lofty truisms ("We will delight our customers") or simple financial targets ("We will grow revenues by 20% a year"). Indeed, the development of a common purpose can be a long, complex process.

For instance, IBM, which needed to reorient its employees from a focus on selling "big iron" in the 1990s, spent a decade building a shared understanding of integrated solutions and on-demand customer focus that went beyond simplistic rhetoric. For many years middle managers and technical employees had found it difficult to frame these concepts in practical terms. They didn't understand at an operational level what it meant for the company to offer not just its own products but those of other vendors—and to sell customers not simply what IBM offered but exactly what they needed when they needed it. Today these common purposes have become part of the language shared daily by people from different functions and at various levels of IBM as they face challenges together.

Properly understood, a shared purpose is a powerful organizing principle. Take, for example, e-Solutions, a unit of about 150 people formed in April 2000 within the cash-management division of Citibank to address a competitive threat from AOL, whose customers were already banking, trading stocks, and buying mutual funds online. To meet this challenge, Citibank sought to boost the growth rate of its core cash-management and trade business from 4% to roughly 20%.

But that was just the business goal. The common purpose behind that number was the aspiration to be a leader in creating new and complex online banking products that could be tailored rapidly to customers' needs. To fully grasp this purpose required widespread discussion and a shared understanding of the company's competitive position within the industry, the evolution of customer needs, and the distinctive capabilities of the organization.

A shared purpose is not the verbiage on a poster or in a document, and it doesn't come via charismatic leaders' pronouncements. It is multidimensional, practical, and constantly enriched in debates about concrete problems. Therefore, when we asked managers at e-Solutions why they worked on a given project, they did not answer "Because that's my job" or "That's where the money is." They talked instead about how the project would advance the shared purpose.

An Ethic of Contribution

Collaborative communities share a distinctive set of values, which we call an *ethic of contribution*. It accords the highest value to people who look beyond their specific roles and advance the common purpose.

The collaborative view rejects the notion of merely "doing a good job," unless that actually makes a contribution. We have learned from practically a century of experience with the traditional model that it is quite possible for everyone to work hard as an individual without producing a good collective result. An ethic of contribution means going beyond one's formal responsibilities to solve broader problems, not just applying greater effort. It also rejects the strong individualism of the market model and instead emphasizes working within the group (rather than trying to gain individual control or responsibility) and eliciting the best contributions from each member for the common good.

Consider the way the software engineers at CSC view the aptly named Capability Maturity Model. "A more mature process means you go from freedom to do things your own way to being critiqued," one engineer acknowledges. "It means going from chaos to structure." That structure makes these knowledge workers more conscious of their interdependence, which has in turn encouraged the shift from an ethic of individual creativity to an ethic of contribution. Another engineer uses this analogy:

"It's a bit like street ball versus NBA basketball. Street ball is roughhousing, showing off. You play for yourself rather than the team, and you do it for the love of the game. In professional basketball, you're part of a team, and you practice a lot together, doing drills and playing practice games. You aren't doing it just for yourself or even just for your team: Other people are involved—managers, lawyers, agents, advertisers. It's a business, not just a game."

The type of trust engendered by an ethic of contribution is less of a given than the trust at traditional organizations, which is firmly rooted in a shared set of rules expressed through tokens of the shared culture. (For many years at IBM, for example, all "good" employees wore the same kind of hat.) But it is also less mercurial than trust built upon faith in a charismatic leader and dazzling displays of individual brilliance. Trust in collaborative communities arises from the degree to which each member believes the other members of the group are able and willing to further the shared purpose. (See the sidebar "Three Models of Corporate Community.")

Given this difference in values, people working on collaborative efforts within larger organizations can find themselves at odds with both the loyalists and the free agents in their midst. For instance, contributors at e-Solutions, working within the generally traditional Citibank organization, were suspicious of the tendency to discuss "who you know" rather than focusing on the task at hand.

"Everyone has their own signals that they look for," said one contributor. "If someone comes into the first meeting and starts throwing around names, my hackles go up because that means, rather than focusing on capabilities and market proposition, they're trying to establish credibility in terms of who they know and who they've talked to. . . . That, at the end of the day, doesn't move you an inch down the line."

Instituting Interdependent Processes

Of course, a shared purpose is meaningless if people with different skills and responsibilities can't contribute to it and to one another. Although traditional bureaucracies excel at vertical coordination, they are not good at encouraging horizontal relations. Free-agent communities excel at ad hoc collaboration but are less successful at large-scale interdependent efforts.

The key coordinating mechanism of a collaborative community, which is often made up of overlapping teams, is a process for aligning the shared purpose within and across the projects. We call that type of coordination *interdependent process management,* a family of techniques including *kaizen,* process mapping, and formal protocols for brainstorming, participatory meeting management, and decision making with multiple stakeholders. CMM, with its well-developed methods, for instance, enables CSC's software engineers to quickly tailor proven project-management procedures to the needs of the project at hand.

Interdependent process management is explicit, flexible, and interactive. Processes are carefully worked out and generally written into protocols, but they are revised continually as the demands of the work and of clients change. They are shaped more by people involved in the task than by those at the top. As one CSC project manager put it, "People support what they help create. . . . As a project manager, you're too far away from the technical work to define the [processes] yourself. . . . It's only by involving your key people that you can be confident you have good [procedures] that have credibility in the eyes of their peers."

At e-Solutions, interdependence took shape in the "e-busi map," which was made available online to everyone in the tion, served as a template for emerging projects, and was c

A Collaborative Dance at Kaiser Permanente

A UNIT OF KAISER PERMANENTE in California developed a new protocol—dubbed the Total Joint Dance—that illustrates how collaborative communities mobilize the knowledge of many diverse contributors to yield scalable business results.

In 2008 Irvine Medical Center wanted to streamline its costliest, most time-intensive surgeries: total-hip and knee-joint replacements. The task was daunting, because the solution required collaboration among specialists who normally fight for resources.

The feat could not have been accomplished by either a traditional or a free-agent type of organization. As Dr. Tadashi Funahashi, the chief of orthopedics, explained, "You have multiple surgeons from multiple different practices, each wanting to do it their own way." What's more, most of Kaiser's employees and insurance customers are unionized. Union cooperation was critical, so neither a top-down administrative mandate nor a surgeon-driven approach was feasible. Kaiser's collaborative community was formalized in the Labor Management Partnership, a joint governance structure involving management and most of Kaiser's employee unions.

In May 2008 a team of OR nurses, surgeons, technicians, and others was assembled. Together this group of union staff, management, and physicians examined every point in the process.

"Usually when we're in the room, we wish it would be done differently," said an OR nurse who was part of the efficiency team. "But this time we actually got a voice in how it's done differently."

Efficiencies were gained by making three types of changes. The first identified parts of the sequential process that could be done simultaneously. Housekeeping staff, for instance, might start the clean-up process when a surgeon begins securing sutures instead of waiting until the patient is out of the operating room.

updated and refined. Emerging teams developed their own maps to feed into it as they defined their roles and responsibilities.

In a collaborative community, anyone can initiate changes if his or her work demands it, but considerable discussion is required to figure out the consequences for other participants and to make sure

The second type of change was triggers: cues to a staff member about when to begin a specific task, such as alerting the post-op and transporting departments that a surgery is ending and the patient will be ready for transport in 15 minutes. This matter might sound trivial, but it requires people to think beyond their own jobs to how their roles fit with others'.

The third change was investing in a "floater" nurse who could move between ORs to provide extra help or relieve staff on breaks. That added capacity is costly but pays off in cycle-time reductions—a trade-off that managers miss if they're focused purely on dollars.

The effect of combining better coordination with increased resources was "like night and day," as Dr. Funahashi describes it. "It's the difference between a well-organized, choreographed team and things happening in a default chaotic state."

With these three changes in place, the number of total-hip and knee-joint replacement surgeries increased from one or two up to four a day, and the average turnaround time between procedures dropped from 45 to 20 minutes. Better coordination freed up 188 hours of OR time a year, at an average annual saving of $132,000 per OR.

Patients and employees are also happier with the outcomes. Surveys of OR staff at one Kaiser facility showed an 85% increase in job satisfaction after the new protocol was adopted.

Perhaps most significant from an organizational perspective is that the gains were scalable. For example, the practices have been adopted by general surgery, along with head and neck, urology, vascular, and other surgery specialties at Irvine. And this approach has spread to other Kaiser hospitals.

that everyone understands them. A Citibank e-Solutions manager described it this way:

"Who owns the process map? We all do. All of us have different perspectives, either on particular partners or on the products or on the overall relationship. When we make a change, it gets communicated

Three Models of Corporate Community

TRADITIONAL ENTERPRISES INSPIRE institutional loyalty; free-agent communities foster individualism. Neither type of organization creates the conditions for collaborative trust that business today requires.

Traditional Industrial Model
These densely interconnected communities are bound by strongly shared values and traditions: clear roles, consistent opportunity for advancement, job security, and benefits. The combination of loyalty and bureaucratic structure allows such organizations to reach unprecedented scale but makes them inflexible and slow to innovate.

Free-Agent Model
These organizations are innovative and flexible. They forgo rules, procedures, and deferential relations in favor of individual effort and reward. Loyalties are based on affection for charismatic leaders. This model is effective for modular projects, but weak organizational ties make it difficult to build the extensive team structure that is needed for knowledge-based work.

Collaborative Community Model
These communities are organized around a sense of shared purpose and coordinated through collaboratively developed, carefully documented procedures. They believe that diversity of capability stimulates innovation. Such organizations excel at interdependent knowledge-based work.

---

to everybody. We've had team meetings to discuss it; everyone understands his role. Originally it was just me and a couple of other people; when we split responsibilities from delivery and execution, we had to redo the exercise."

This kind of process management is tough to maintain. It requires people who are accustomed to more-traditional systems to develop radically new habits. In either bureaucratic or market-oriented organizations, people are given objectives and procedures but are generally left alone to operate within those boundaries. Collaborative process management intrudes on that autonomy—it requires people to continually adapt to others' needs. Accepting the value of this interdependence is often difficult, and the habits of documentation and discussion may require considerable time to take root. A manager at Johnson & Johnson described his group's struggles:

"The team acknowledged problems of poor alignment. As a result, we sat down as a team and put things on a piece of paper. The idea was that I could just go back and refer to something we had decided and say, 'On May 15th we decided x, y, and z.' Within a day, that plan was obsolete. We were making agreements, changing dates, reprioritizing, and not updating the document. The main problem is the informal side conversations between two people. They make a decision without informing the rest of the team. The key is to review this periodically as things change. We need to update and maintain the document as we have conversations."

Creating a Collaborative Infrastructure

If work is organized in teams and workers increasingly serve on more than one team, the need for a new type of authority structure arises—one that involves overlapping spheres of influence. We call it *participative centralization*. It's participative because the collaborative enterprise seeks to mobilize everyone's knowledge; it's centralized because that knowledge must be coordinated so that it can be applied at scale. An e-Solutions contributor described a typical example:

"There are really three heads of the unit. One of them is responsible for my salary, but from a professional perspective they're equally important. One of them tells me more what to do on a tactical level, another more on general direction and vision. The advantage is that there are multiple people who can play multiple roles, so we can get at resources from multiple perspectives. In the e-space it's very useful to be nimble in that way. At the end of the day it is clear who gets to make the decision, but it rarely comes to that. I wouldn't say that decisions are never bumped up; I would say that these flat structures invite more questioning and more discussion, which I think is a good thing because when you have a stricter organizational hierarchy, people are more reluctant to bring things to their superiors."

If what this contributor describes appears to be a matrix, it is. The matrix structure has been tried by many firms during recent decades, and its failure rate is high, so people often assume it's a poor model. But matrix structures actually offer a huge competitive advantage precisely because they are so hard to sustain. They both support and are supported by the other features of the collaborative model: shared purpose, an ethic of collaboration, and interdependent process management. Without those buttresses, the matrix model collapses under the weight of political bickering.

Pay systems are not primary drivers of motivation in collaborative organizations. People will become dissatisfied over time if they feel their pay does not reflect their contributions, but their daily decision making is not guided by the goal of maximizing their compensation. Rather, the operative motivation is what Tracy Kidder, in *The Soul of a New Machine,* memorably labeled the "pinball" theory of management: If you win, you get to play again—to take on a new challenge, to move to a new level. More broadly, people talk about one another's contributions a lot, so collaborative communities foster a relatively accurate reputational system, which becomes the basis for selecting people to participate in new and interesting projects.

That said, pay systems need to be equitable. Given that formal supervisors can't monitor everything that subordinates in different departments are doing on various projects, collaborative organizations rely heavily on some form of multisource, 360-degree feedback.

The Collaborative Revolution

We do not wish to downplay the undeniable challenges of building collaborative communities. Setting and aligning processes that interconnect people on many teams requires constant attention. Not every star player you may wish to attract will want to relinquish autonomy to reap the rewards of a team's effort. Allocating pay fairly according to contribution is tricky.

Indeed, we have found that the patience and skill required to create and maintain a sense of common purpose are rare in corporate hierarchies, particularly given that it is not a set-it-and-forget-it process. The purpose must be continually redefined as markets and clients evolve, and members of the community need to be constantly engaged in shaping and understanding complex collective missions. That kind of participation is costly and time-consuming. And charismatic leaders who believe that they should simply go with their gut often don't relish this way of doing business.

What's more, developing a collaborative community, as IBM's experience attests, is a long-term investment, in tension with many short-term competitive and financial pressures that companies must navigate. So we do not envision a day anytime soon when all companies will be organized entirely into collaborative communities.

Still, few would argue that today's market imperative—to innovate fast enough to keep up with the competition and with customer needs while simultaneously improving cost and efficiency—can be met without the active engagement of employees in different functions and at multiple levels of responsibility. To undertake that endeavor, businesses need a lot more than minimal cooperation and mere compliance. They need everyone's ideas on how to do things better and more cheaply. They need true collaboration.

A century ago a few companies struggled to build organizations reliable enough to take advantage of the emerging mass consumer economy. Those that succeeded became household names: General Motors, DuPont, Standard Oil. Today reliability is no longer a key competitive advantage, and we are at a new turning point. The organizations that will become the household names of this century will be renowned for sustained, large-scale, efficient innovation. The key to that capability is neither company loyalty nor free-agent autonomy but, rather, a strong collaborative community.

Originally published in July–August 2011. Reprint R1107G

Silo Busting

How to Execute on the Promise of Customer Focus.
by Ranjay Gulati

IN 2001, UNDER PRICE pressure from the government and managed health care organizations, GE Medical Systems (now GE Healthcare) created a unit, Performance Solutions, to sell consulting services packaged with imaging equipment as integrated solutions. These solutions, priced at a premium, were intended to enhance productivity by, for instance, reducing patient backlogs. At the time, lots of companies were making the move from selling products to selling solutions in an attempt to differentiate themselves in increasingly commoditized markets.

GE's plan seemed to work well at first. The Performance Solutions unit enjoyed strong initial revenues, in part because most new contracts included additional consulting services valued at $25,000 to $50,000. And the unit had some notable successes. It helped Stanford University Medical Center, for example, make the transition to an all-digital imaging environment at its adult hospital, children's medical center, and an outpatient facility—moves that delivered millions of dollars in new revenues for the medical center and substantial cost savings.

But by 2005, the unit's growth had begun a swift decline. It turned out that equipment salespeople had trouble explaining the value of consulting services, so when they called on customers they couldn't contribute much to the sale of additional services. What's more, these reps were reluctant to allow Performance Solutions salespeople to contact their customers. And by marketing the unit's consulting services with its product portfolio, GE generated solutions that were useful for customers whose problems could clearly be solved using GE's equipment but less compelling for those whose needs were linked only loosely to the imaging products.

In the end, GE refashioned the unit to address customers' needs in a more comprehensive fashion and to better align the sales organization. For instance, the majority of solutions now focus mainly on consulting services and are no longer marketed only with GE equipment. The solutions group secured new contracts valued at more than $500 million in 2006. But in trying to escape the perils of commoditization, the company initially fell into a classic trap: It was seeking to solve customer problems but was viewing those problems through the lens of its own products, rather than from the customer's perspective. It was pulling together what it had on offer in the hope that customers would value the whole more than the sum of its parts.

Over the past five years, I have studied the challenge of top- and bottom-line growth in the face of commoditization, and I have found that many companies make the same mistake. They profess the importance of shifting from products to solutions—in fact, in a survey of senior executives I conducted a few years ago, more than two-thirds of the respondents cited this shift as a strategic priority in the next decade. But their knowledge and expertise are housed within organizational silos, and they have trouble harnessing their resources across those internal boundaries in a way that customers truly value and are willing to pay for.

Some notable exceptions have emerged: companies that, like GE, found ways to transcend those silos in the interest of customer needs. By the late 1990s, for instance, Best Buy had nearly saturated the market with store openings and was facing increased competition not just from other retailers like Wal-Mart but from suppliers such as Dell. It tried to spark growth through various marketing approaches, but the company's efforts didn't take off until it launched a major initiative to restructure around customer solutions. Between 2000 and 2005, Best Buy's stock price grew at an annual rate of almost 30%.

Idea in Brief

For many senior executives, shifting from selling products to selling solutions—packages of products and services—is a priority in today's increasingly commoditized markets. Companies, however, aren't always structured to make that shift. Knowledge and expertise often reside in silos, and many companies have trouble harnessing their resources across those boundaries in a way that customers value and are willing to pay for. Some companies—like GE Healthcare, Best Buy, and commercial real estate provider Jones Lang LaSalle (JLL)—have restructured themselves around customer needs to deliver true solutions. They did so by engaging in four sets of activities. **Coordination**—to deliver customer-focused solutions, three things must occur easily across boundaries: information sharing, division of labor, and decision making. Sometimes this involves replacing traditional silos with customer-focused ones, but more often it entails transcending existing boundaries. JLL has experimented with both approaches. **Cooperation**—customer-centric companies, such as Cisco Systems, develop metrics for customer satisfaction and incentives that reward customer-focused cooperation. Most also shake up the power structure so that people who are closest to customers have the authority to act on their behalf. **Capability**—delivering customer-focused solutions requires some employees to be generalists instead of specialists. They need experience with more than one product or service, a deep knowledge of customer needs, and the ability to traverse internal boundaries. **Connection**—by combining their offerings with those of a partner, companies can cut costs even as they create higher-value solutions, as Starbucks has found through its diverse partnerships. To stand out in a commoditized market, companies must understand what customers value. Ultimately, some customers may be better off purchasing products and services piecemeal.

Commercial real estate provider Jones Lang LaSalle (JLL), under serious price competition, made a similar strategic shift in 2001, when its large customers began demanding integrated real estate services. For instance, corporate customers wanted the same people who found or built property for them to manage it. In response, JLL adopted a solutions-oriented structure that helped attract numerous large and highly profitable new accounts.

For GE Healthcare, Best Buy, and JLL, as well as for other companies I have studied, the journey to understand and unite around customer needs was a multiyear endeavor with major challenges and setbacks along the way. The effort required systematic, ongoing change to help organizations transcend existing product-based or geographic silos and, in some cases, replace them with customer-oriented ones. In particular, I found that successful companies engaged in four sets of activities:

- **Coordination.** Establishing structural mechanisms and processes that allow employees to improve their focus on the customer by harmonizing information and activities across units.

- **Cooperation.** Encouraging people in all parts of the company—through cultural means, incentives, and the allocation of power—to work together in the interest of customer needs.

- **Capability development.** Ensuring that enough people in the organization have the skills to deliver customer-focused solutions and defining a clear career path for employees with those skills.

- **Connection.** Developing relationships with external partners to increase the value of solutions cost effectively.

The first three sets of activities mutually reinforce the effort to put customers at the organization's fore; the fourth dramatically increases the power and reach of solutions by focusing attention beyond the firm's boundaries. All of them help companies transcend internal silos in service of higher-value customer solutions.

Coordination for Customer Focus

As GE Healthcare quickly discovered, it's easy to say that you offer solutions; salespeople may readily seize the concept as their newest product. But I've found that few companies are actually structured to deliver products and services in a synchronized way that's attractive from a customer's perspective. Individual units are historically focused on perfecting their products and processes, and give little thought to how their offerings might be even more valuable to the end user when paired with those of another unit. It's not just that the status quo doesn't reward collaborative behavior—although the right incentives are also critical. It's that the connections literally aren't in place.

One way to forge those connections is to do away with traditional silos altogether and create new ones organized by customer segments or needs. Many companies, however, are understandably reluctant to let go of the economies of scale and depth of knowledge and expertise associated with non-customer-focused silos. A company organized around geographies can customize offerings to suit local preferences, for instance, while a technology-centric firm can be quick to market with technical innovations. In many cases, functional and geographic silos were created precisely to help companies coordinate such activities as designing innovative products or gaining geographic focus. A customer focus requires them to emphasize a different set of activities and coordinate them in a different way.

In their initial attempts to offer customer solutions, companies are likely to create structures and processes that transcend rather than obliterate silos. Such boundary-spanning efforts may be highly informal—even as simple as hoping for or encouraging serendipity and impromptu conversations that lead to unplanned cross-unit solutions. But the casual exchange of information and ideas is generally most effective among senior executives, who have a better understanding than their subordinates of corporate goals and easier access to other leaders in the organization.

One way to achieve more-formal coordination without discarding existing silos is to layer boundary-spanning roles or units over the current structure and charge them with connecting the company's disparate activities to customer needs. JLL, which was created by the 1999 merger of LaSalle Partners and Jones Lang Wootton, had organized the corporate side of its business in the Americas into three units, each offering a particular service: representing tenants who wished to lease or purchase, maintaining

The Four Cs of Customer-Focused Solutions

COMPANIES LOOKING TO GROW in a commoditized marketplace like to say that they offer customer solutions: strategic packages of products and services that are hard to copy and can command premium prices. But most companies aren't set up to deliver solutions that customers truly value. Successful companies make significant changes in four areas to deliver real solutions.

Coordination

In most companies, knowledge and expertise reside in distinct units—organized by product, service, or geography. To deliver customer-focused solutions, companies need mechanisms that allow customer-related information sharing, division of labor, and decision making to occur easily across company boundaries. Sometimes this involves completely obliterating established silos and replacing them with silos organized around the customer, but more often it entails using structures and processes to transcend existing boundaries.

Cooperation

Customer-centric companies use both substance and symbolism to foster a culture of customer-focused cooperation. They develop metrics that measure, for instance, customer satisfaction and incentives that reward customer-focused behavior, even if it sacrifices unit performance. Most also shake up

---

buildings and properties, and managing real estate development. Each unit had authority over what services to offer, at what price, and to which clients. The units also had profit-and-loss responsibility for their respective businesses.

In 2001 the firm began to hear complaints from such large corporate clients as Bank of America that buying real estate services piecemeal from numerous companies and interacting with relatively junior salespeople were taking up too much executive time. One client explained, "We like him [the ad hoc account manager], but he is too low on the totem pole." At the time, many *Fortune* 500 companies were starting to outsource all real estate management. In response, JLL created an umbrella group, Corporate Solutions, that

the power structure so that people who are closest to customers have the authority to act on their behalf.

Capability

Delivering customer-focused solutions requires at least some employees to have two kinds of generalist skills. The first is experience with more than one product or service, along with a deep knowledge of customer needs (multidomain skills), and the second is an ability to traverse internal boundaries (boundary-spanning skills). In many companies, especially those organized around products, employees aren't rewarded for being generalists. Organizations that succeed in delivering solutions, however, invest significant time and resources in developing generalists. Furthermore, they establish clear career pathways for those who pursue the generalist route.

Connection

By redefining the boundaries of the company in order to connect more tightly with external partners, companies can not only cut costs by outsourcing all but core activities (and perhaps even by finding ways to outsource them) but also create higher-value solutions by combining their offerings with those of a complementary partner. Working with other companies still means crossing boundaries, but in this instance the boundaries are between a company and its partners.

comprised the three service units as well as an account management function, which served as a point of contact for large corporate customers. The account management group was staffed with high-ranking officers who had the authority to negotiate the pricing and delivery of real estate solutions, and the experience to help clients with strategic planning. By approaching Bank of America with a dedicated, senior-level account manager, JLL addressed the customer's complaint and was rewarded with one of just two spots (reduced from five) as a provider of outsourced services for the bank's 65 million square feet of U.S. real estate. Thus began a tremendous run that saw JLL's solutions revenue in the Americas grow more than 50% between 2002 and 2005.

Cisco Systems took a similar, layered approach to customer focus, but with a twist. The company, which had been organized by customer segment from 1997 to 2001, reverted to a technology-focused structure after the Internet bubble burst, forcing the company to address costly redundancies. Under its previous structure, Cisco had been creating the same or similar products for different customer segments, whose needs often overlapped. In fact, in some cases each line of business offered its own technology or solution for the same problem.

However, leaders feared that organizing around technologies, which involved centralizing marketing and R&D, would distance Cisco from customers' requirements. The answer was to retain the company's three sales groups based on customer type but establish a central marketing organization—residing between the technology groups and the customer-facing sales units—responsible for, among other things, facilitating the integration of products and technologies. The marketing group also established a cross-silo solutions-engineering team to bring disparate technologies together in a lab, test them, and create blueprints for end-user solutions. In addition to those structural measures, Cisco implemented several customer-focused processes, such as a customer champion program, which assigned senior executives as advocates for important customers. CEO John Chambers, for instance, was designated Ford's champion in 2002. In 2004 the company supplemented its advocates with cross-functional leadership teams organized by customer type, mimicking the previous structure, at least at the senior management level. Those teams—described by one executive as "the voice of the customer"—oversee six end-to-end processes that cut across functional boundaries such as quote-to-cash (the order cycle) and issue-to-resolution (technical support).

While bridging mechanisms such as cross-silo teams and processes can be very effective, they aren't easy to implement. A history of independence often leads to protectionist behavior. At JLL, for instance, business unit managers were initially reluctant to cede decision-making authority to account managers, particularly ones who lacked experience with that unit's service. Conflicts also arose over pricing and account managers' compensation. What's more, while JLL's Corporate Solutions group had positioned the firm well to meet the increasing demands of corporate real estate customers, single-transaction customers considered the relatively small number of JLL account managers in local markets to be a problem. Those customers wanted professionals who could negotiate the best deal and execute entire transactions. As JLL discovered, the benefits of bundled solutions wear off if customers perceive a weakness in any component. Ultimately, JLL's layered approach to silo busting was still limiting the firm's growth.

To dispense with such tensions, JLL next took the more dramatic and highly formal measure of silo swapping—a wholesale, permanent structural shift to spin internal groups and processes around a customer axis. That is, it swapped its current, service-focused silos for those structured explicitly around the customer to maximize company-customer synergies. As part of that process, it replaced the account management function and the three service silos that had resided within the Corporate Solutions group with two organizations denoted simply Clients and Markets, a restructuring that put more people in the field, closer to clients, and focused all internal groups and processes on customer needs. The Markets organization handled one-off transactions, represented JLL's full range of offerings to those customers, and provided local support for larger clients. As accounts grew, they were assigned an account manager from the Clients organization, which was composed primarily of account teams managing the firm's relationships with large, multiservice customers. These teams were considered profit centers and so had the authority to hire and terminate employees. To preserve its product and service expertise without a product- and service-based structure, JLL embedded service specialists within account teams in both organizations and created a product management team charged with keeping offerings competitive. It's too soon to know how well the customer-focused silos are working, and the firm may face new, unanticipated challenges, but early results look promising: In the past year, revenues have increased by 30% and profits by almost 60%.

Culture of Cooperation

While coordination mechanisms can align tasks and information around customers' needs, they don't necessarily inspire a willingness among members of competing silos to fully cooperate and make sometimes time-consuming and costly adjustments in the interest of customers. Just as important as coordination, then, is a cooperative environment in which people are rewarded for busting through silos to deliver customer solutions. Customer-centric companies live by a set of values that put the customer front and center, and they reinforce those values through cultural elements, power structures, metrics, and incentives that reward customer-focused, solutions-oriented behavior.

Many product-centric companies probably start out with a focus on customers, aiming to design products with broad appeal. But after early successes, they internalize and institutionalize the notion that markets respond primarily to great products and services. Decisions and behaviors, including those related specifically to customers, are then viewed through the lens of the product. Quality, for example, is defined by meeting internal standards rather than customer requirements. Over time, even the sales and marketing departments lose their customer focus, as product successes dominate company lore. In this way, the company develops a pervasive inside-out perspective.

In contrast, customer-focused companies, even those in technology-intensive arenas, build an outside-in perspective into all major elements of their cultures. They hold solving customer problems above all else and celebrate customer-oriented victories. At Cisco, technical innovation is clearly valued. The drive to solve customer problems fuels that innovation no matter where it leads the company, a mind-set that is reflected in the statement on all employee badges, "No Technology Religion." As one manager said, "Being able to listen carefully to create relevancy [for customers] is a more important business value than innovation." In line with this thinking, Cisco puts a relatively large number of employees in direct contact with customers, including groups such as human resources that typically don't interact with customers.

It helped that Cisco had the luxury of an existing culture of customer focus. Cofounder Sandy Lerner, in the company's earliest days, invented a customized multiprotocol router for a customer who initially found no Cisco products that met his needs. From then on, Lerner made it her mission to establish a culture where everybody, even those in units distant from customers, went beyond providing standard customer support to addressing specific problems. Consequently, even when the company reorganized its silos away from the customer in 2001, it was able to maintain enough interaction among units to ensure a customer-centric view.

At least half the battle of promoting cross-silo, customer-focused cooperation lies in the "softer" aspects of culture, including values and the way the company communicates them through images, symbols, and stories. Touting service accomplishments instead of, or at least in addition to, product accomplishments through company lore can begin to shift people's mind-sets. Cisco's employee badges broadcast a focus on customer needs, as does a well-known company legend about how Chambers was 30 minutes late to his first board meeting because he chose to take a call from an irate customer. Linguistic conventions may also be used to signify the value of the customer: Target and Disney refer to customers as "guests."

Another admittedly soft but powerful cultural tool for aligning employees around customer needs is to treat your workers the way you want them to treat customers. The hope is that people will adopt a collaborative orientation and customer focus because they want to, not just because they'll reap a financial reward. Cisco is highly egalitarian, reinforcing the notion that all employees are important, which makes them more likely to cooperate across silos. The company offers equal access to parking spaces, for instance, and designates window-facing cubicles for nonmanagement employees, locating supervisors' offices within the interior of the floor.

Of course, the softer cooperation-promoting measures won't take hold if the harder ones—power structures, metrics, and incentives—don't reinforce them. Power structures are notoriously difficult to change. For example, in a customer-centric environment, people who are close to the customer and adept at building bridges across silos should gain power and prominence; but unit leaders responsible for products or geographies who had clout in the old organization won't hand over their customer relationships and concomitant power bases without a struggle.

That was the case at JLL. Before the company created the Corporate Solutions organization, power resided almost exclusively within the service-based business units. Even after the account manager position was instituted, final pricing authority rested with the units, which made it difficult to compete with multiservice packages. Although solutions ideally carry a premium price, JLL's initial intent was to better serve customers' needs by simplifying the management of real estate and to position the firm as a multiservice provider. However, when JLL created a package of real estate services, the price quickly mounted, resulting in sticker shock among potential customers, many of whom associated buying in bulk with discount pricing. JLL unit heads—who wanted to maximize their own return, not subsidize other units—refused to budge on prices. In some cases, package proposals were delayed, thanks to negotiations that stalled or ended in a stalemate that could be resolved only by those higher in the organization. In other cases, the packages weren't priced competitively, and the firm lost the business.

The issue of autonomy raised concerns as well. JLL's business units were accustomed to a high degree of independence. They protected their client relationships and had always been wary of introducing other services—even before the account management unit was in place—because delivery would be out of their control and they feared damaging the relationships. JLL took several steps to resolve those tensions. For one, it signaled the importance and value of the account manager role by assigning it to only very senior executives, including two who had achieved the title of international director, a distinction earned by less than 2% of employees. The firm also delivered a series of presentations at annual companywide meetings highlighting the significance of the role to the firm's growth.

To ease the pricing standoffs, JLL began in 2003 to allow account managers to provide input into the performance evaluations of business unit employees who touched their clients. At the same time, JLL took steps to retain some power and recognition for the business unit CEOs and, in the process, help them learn more about the services outside their silos and how they might gain personally from cross-unit sales. Unit CEOs, for example, were asked to oversee accounts on which their services were a particularly important component; in this role, unit heads were explicitly responsible for the performance of account managers. Because their bonuses were tied to the account managers' overall performance, the unit heads developed a clearer picture of the value contributed by services outside their silos. They were also required to meet regularly with customers to discuss their needs and the quality of the firm's service.

To support a shifting power landscape, firms must also embrace new metrics and incentives. The product-focused metrics most companies rely on—revenues, growth, and margins—don't reward cross-silo cooperation or customer centricity. Sales commissions in some organizations encourage managers to bring in new customers rather than nurture existing relationships, for example.

Cisco is relentless about measuring and rewarding employees on the basis of customer-related performance indicators. A Web-based survey helps determine the pre- and post-sale satisfaction of customers who buy directly from Cisco or indirectly through resellers. Survey questions focus on a customer's overall experience with and perceptions of Cisco, along with product-specific issues. Follow-up surveys with some customers explore their experiences with certain products more deeply. All bonuses are tied directly to these customer satisfaction data, so employees are encouraged to cooperate across internal boundaries. Moreover, all employees, including interns and part-timers, are eligible for stock options.

Building Capability

Regardless of the incentives and cultural elements in place to enhance customer-focused silo busting, employees will fall back on their old competencies and ways of thinking if they haven't developed new skills. For example, even though one of the companies I studied told product salespeople to include new consulting-based offerings in their pitches to customers, the reps found it easier to give a superficial account of the new offerings or to omit them from their pitches altogether. Old habits die hard.

As a company becomes more adept at inducing coordination and cooperation across units, new skills become valued and desirable. Rather than highly specialized expertise, customer-focused solutions require employees to develop two kinds of skills: multidomain skills (the ability to work with multiple products and services, which requires a deep understanding of customers' needs) and boundary-spanning skills (the ability to forge connections across internal boundaries). Such generalist skills are typically not rewarded or developed in a product-oriented organization, so it's not easy to find customer-facing generalists. The companies that succeed invest significant time and resources in developing generalists. Furthermore, they map clear career paths for those who pursue this route.

At JLL, most of the first account managers had spent the majority of their careers in a single service unit within the firm and remained members of that unit even after becoming account managers. Consequently, they were not always deeply acquainted with the other businesses or able to manage service bundles skillfully. Account managers hired from the outside were generally chosen for their ability to execute real estate transactions, not for the breadth of their service knowledge.

To foster the development of boundary-spanning skills and cultivate a cadre of employees who could grow into the account manager role, JLL began to rotate individuals through the three remaining silos (before swapping the service silos for customer silos), forcing them to acquire greater knowledge of the products, services, and capabilities of each unit, as well as to expand their personal networks across the firm. For those already in account management roles, the company instituted training sessions through regular conference calls and meetings. Early sessions tackled relatively simple tasks, such as the establishment of a common vocabulary. Subsequent sessions focused on improving account managers' knowledge of each unit's offerings and on cross-silo sales skills and new metrics, including the first rudimentary client-based profit-and-loss statements. An unanticipated benefit of the training was that it brought the account managers together regularly, helping them to stop identifying only with their silos and to begin forming a group identity that enhanced their cross-silo networks. As a natural consequence, top management could see that account managers were assuming increased responsibility for a broader range of services.

Best Buy's shift to solutions selling entailed identifying and targeting five large, profitable customer segments: young, tech-savvy adults; busy and affluent professionals; family men; busy, suburban moms; and small-business customers. Each store was designed to suit the needs of its largest customer segment. A "busy mom" store, for instance, features personal shopping assistance and a kid-friendly layout. Stores targeting the tech-savvy offer higher-end consumer electronics and separate showrooms for high-definition home theater systems. When the company rolled out its customer-centric strategy, it conducted extensive training to help employees understand their store's particular customer segment. It also trained sales associates on basic financial metrics to highlight how their efforts on behalf of target customers affect store performance.

At the corporate level, Best Buy created a Customer Centricity University for senior officers who had not been involved with planning the new strategy. For those executives, Best Buy outlined the rationale for the new approach, including detailed financials, and held breakout sessions with the teams responsible for developing and executing the strategy for each customer segment. Over 11 months, all employees and contractors residing at headquarters, as well as many other corporate employees, participated in the program. It was then disbanded, its essential elements incorporated into the company's orientation program for new employees.

Enhancing skill sets is only part of the challenge of capability building. Companies must also develop attractive career paths that give emerging generalist stars a sense of identity and a clear route for advancement. Even specialists whose roles may not change much in the new organization will probably have to develop some generalist skills and learn how these could contribute to their advancement. JLL, for instance, at first had difficulty attracting candidates for account manager positions, largely because the firm had measured success and offered promotions on the basis of achievements within a unit. Job security was a major concern for potential account managers, as one of the first to hold the position explains: "One of the big fears was that these accounts don't last forever. So if a person left his or her specialized area of expertise to run an account and after three years . . . the firm was no longer providing services for that account, employees feared that that person would be out of a job."

JLL addressed the career path issue in part through its customer-focused reorganization—whereby the Clients group housed account managers in a well-defined unit with a clear career trajectory. Other firms have developed "talent marketplaces" to signal the value they place on generalist, cross-silo skills. Modeled after informal marketplaces used within law firms, academia, and R&D units, these forums match employees on a flexible basis with available positions or assignments, thereby allowing generalist and specialist career tracks to coexist.

Connection with External Partners

The three factors we've discussed—coordination, cooperation, and capability building—are silo-busting tactics that align business units around a customer axis. But by redefining the boundaries of the company itself, firms can further fight commoditization in two ways: cutting costs by outsourcing all but core activities (and, in some cases, by finding creative ways to outsource them) and joining forces with companies that have complementary offerings to create even higher-value solutions, which command a larger price premium. Such approaches still require cross-boundary efforts, but the boundaries are between a company and its partners.

Starbucks continues to charge a premium for coffee, previously a commodity product, and exponentially increase the company's sales through intercompany relationships that keep costs low while expanding the firm's offerings. It chooses suppliers very carefully (quality and service take priority over cost) and then shares an unusual amount of financial information, using a two-way, open-book costing model that allows suppliers to see the company's margins and Starbucks to review the vendors' costs. In return, the company expects suppliers to treat it as a preferred customer in terms of pricing, profit percentage, and the resources committed to the partnership.

As for expanding its offerings, Starbucks seeks to enrich the customer experience through alliances with partners in a variety of industries. Its bottled Frappuccino beverage is manufactured, distributed, and marketed through a 50/50 joint venture with PepsiCo; its ice cream is made and distributed by Dreyer's; its supermarket coffees are marketed and distributed by Kraft, one of the company's main competitors in the at-home coffee consumption market. A more recent alliance with Jim Beam Brands brought Starbucks into a new drink category: spirits. In 2005, the two companies launched Starbucks Cream Liqueur, which is sold in liquor stores, restaurants, and bars, but not in coffeehouses.

Starbucks's boundary-expanding moves have extended to non-consumable items as well. For several years, customers have been able to buy CDs at the stores, and the company recently began to promote movies as part of its ongoing efforts to become, according to the *New York Times,* a "purveyor of premium-blend culture." It sponsors discussion groups (with free coffee) and is considering selling DVDs, publishing new authors, and producing films. To coordinate these promotions and partnerships, Starbucks has formed an entertainment division with offices in Seattle and Los Angeles.

Finally, Starbucks has expanded internationally by leveraging not other companies' products and services but the capabilities of regional partners. Whereas the company owns most of its domestic retail stores, it allows foreign companies to own and operate Starbucks stores in markets where those players are already established. In 1995 Japanese specialty retailer Sazaby opened a Starbucks in Tokyo. In such cases, Starbucks provides operating expertise and control through licensing, while the foreign partners take on financial risk and advise Starbucks on real estate, regulations, suppliers, labor, and culture in the markets they know best. Sharing responsibilities in this way requires Starbucks to apply the principles of coordination, cooperation, and capability building to its external relationships.

Starbucks's relationship-building capability has enabled the company to grow far faster than it could have on its own. What's more, with just about every fast-food company selling premium coffee, and versatile and affordable new coffeemakers lining the shelves at Target, the company has been able to shore up its position by selling not just coffee but a coffeehouse experience, built largely around a series of partnerships and alliances that provide customers with an array of high-quality offerings.

Such relationships can be mutually reinforcing: As one company shrinks operations to cut costs—seeking partners to take on formerly in-house activities—its suppliers must expand their horizons by increasing the range of their offerings or finding their own partners to help them do this. IBM, even while taking over major back-office operations for large companies, has condensed its own core operations by outsourcing activities like repair and server manufacturing to contractors such as Solectron. Solectron, in turn, has expanded its boundaries by acquiring an IBM repair center in the Netherlands, allowing IBM to condense still further.

There are pitfalls to integrating closely with suppliers. Some companies—especially those that are unclear on their core values—give away too much. Others become captive to their key suppliers and lose the motivation to make ongoing investments in new technology. Some also find that they are funding the development expertise and scale that may allow a partner to become a competitor, as when cell phone supplier BenQ moved from making handsets for Motorola to marketing its own brand of handsets in foreign markets where Motorola already had a presence. Integrated partnerships can also be risky if companies put a lot of information into their vendors' hands, as Starbucks does. If trust on either side is eroded, one party could misuse the information.

In managing external relationships to avoid such pitfalls, it makes sense to apply the principles used to manage across internal silos—particularly the principles of coordination and cooperation. The challenges of internal and external execution are not exactly the same, but they share many themes, such as the need to find efficient ways of exchanging information and aligning incentives. So, for instance, Starbucks has a set of formal coordination structures to help information flow between partners. In addition to regular meetings between senior management on both sides, Starbucks has a dedicated training program for employees who will be involved in managing supplier relationships. To ensure that both parties follow clear rules for knowledge sharing, the company has created a handbook for suppliers, which describes the firm's purchasing philosophies and policies, along with the standards vendors must meet on eight criteria.

Cooperation issues may be even more central to external relationships than to internal ones, given the need to apportion value fairly among parties and the omnipresent risk of opportunistic behavior. Cultural fit lays the groundwork for cooperation, and efforts at cultural synchrony may begin even before the partnership does. Starbucks not only conducts a careful assessment of a supplier's brand and operations but also evaluates cultural fit, largely through an event called Discovery Day, when prospective partners come to Seattle to discuss cultural and other commonalities as well as differences between themselves and Starbucks.

In today's ever expanding and shifting business arena, and in light of a growing focus on customer needs, the definitions of what is inside a company and what is outside are no longer clear. But as our sense of firm boundaries evolves, so will our understanding of how best to breach internal and external barriers.

There are few downsides to developing true solutions. The risk is that in the rush to stand out in the crowd, many companies forget that solving customer problems requires a deep knowledge of who their target customers are and what they need. Some customers are better off purchasing products and services piecemeal. Leaders at GE Healthcare originally targeted solutions at large national accounts—which, it turned out, bought largely on price. These clients almost by definition weren't good candidates for the solutions offering. The company consequently refined its target customer profile to focus on multihospital systems—with at least $500 million in annual revenue—that demonstrated a willingness to provide GE with meaningful access to the most-senior executives. Through this targeting, GE Healthcare narrowed its focus to just 150 of the roughly 400 multihospital systems in the U.S. health care market—giving primary attention to 50 accounts that included customers ready to enter into a contractual relationship with GE and those that exhibited many key characteristics and expressed a willingness to work with GE.

The lesson for GE, as for others, is that it doesn't pay to put the solutions cart before the horse of coordinated customer focus. To stand out in a commoditized market, companies must understand what customers truly value. The only way to do that is to break down the traditional, often entrenched, silos and unite resources to focus directly on customer needs.

Originally published in May 2007. Reprint R0705F

Harnessing Your Staff's Informal Networks

by Richard McDermott and Douglas Archibald

IF YOUR SMARTEST EMPLOYEES are getting together to solve problems and develop new ideas on their own, the best thing to do is to stay out of their way, right? Workers can easily share insights electronically, and they often don't want or appreciate executive oversight. Well, think again. Though in-house networks of experts—or "communities of practice"—were once entirely unofficial, today they are increasingly integrated into companies' formal management structures.

Independent, off-the-grid communities have proliferated in recent years, and many companies have counted on them to deliver creative solutions to challenges that bridge functional gaps. But in the past few years, outside forces—technological advances, globalization, increased demands on employees' time—have begun to undermine communities' success. Consider the rise and fall of an informal group of experts at a large water-engineering company located just outside London. Starting in the early 1990s, they began meeting weekly to discuss strategies for designing new water-treatment facilities. The gatherings were so lively and informative that they actually drew crowds of onlookers. (The company can't be named for reasons of confidentiality.)

The community initially thrived because it operated so informally. United by a common professional passion, participants would huddle around conference tables and compare data, trade insights, and argue over which designs would work best with local water systems. And the community achieved results: Participants found ways to significantly cut the time and cost involved in system design by increasing the pool of experience that they could draw upon, tapping insights from different disciplines, and recycling design ideas from other projects.

Too much attention from management, went the thinking, would crush the group's collaborative nature. But the very informality of this community eventually rendered it obsolete. What happened to it was typical: The members gained access to more sophisticated design tools and to vast amounts of data via the internet. Increased global connectivity drew more people into the community and into individual projects. Soon the engineers were spending more time at their desks, gathering and organizing data, sorting through multiple versions of designs, and managing remote contacts. The community started to feel less intimate, and its members, less obligated to their peers. Swamped, the engineers found it difficult to justify time for voluntary meetings. Today the community in effect has dissolved—along with the hopes that it would continue generating high-impact ideas.

Our research has shown that many other communities failed for similar reasons. Nevertheless, communities of practice aren't dead. Many are thriving—you'll find them developing global processes, resolving troubled implementation, and guiding operational efforts. But they differ from their forebears in some important respects. Today they're an actively managed part of the organization, with specific goals, explicit accountability, and clear executive oversight. To get experts to dedicate time to them, companies have to make sure that communities contribute meaningfully to the organization and operate efficiently.

We've observed this shift in our consulting work and in our research. This research was conducted with the Knowledge and Innovation Network at Warwick Business School and funded by the

Idea in Brief

Informal employee networks, or communities of practice, are an inexpensive and efficient way for experts to share knowledge and ideas. But communities work best if they have clear accountability and management oversight.

Effective communities tackle real problems for senior management. At Pfizer, for instance, communities are responsible for helping developers make tough calls on drug-safety issues.

Communities are like teams but focus on the long term. Pfizer's safety communities are assigned organizationwide goals—such as ensuring that safety research uses the latest science—which project teams, focused on specific deliverables, could never meet.

Technology makes global collaboration possible, but successful communities also depend on the human systems—focus, goals, and management attention—that integrate them into the organization.

Warwick Innovative Manufacturing Research Centre and by Schlumberger, an oil-field services company. To examine the health and impact of communities, we did a quantitative study of 52 communities in 10 industries, and a qualitative assessment of more than 140 communities in a dozen organizations, consisting of interviews with support staff, leaders, community members, and senior management.

The communities at construction and engineering giant Fluor illustrate the extent of the change. Global communities have replaced the company's distributed functional structure. While project teams remain the primary organizational unit, 44 discipline- and industry-focused communities, with 24,000 active members, support the teams. The communities provide all functional services—creating guidelines for work practices and procedures; publishing technical documents; and offering career development, access to expert advice, and help with technical questions. They are the first and best source for technical knowledge at Fluor.

Here's one example of how this works: Not long ago, a Fluor nuclear-cleanup project team had to install a soil barrier over a drainage field once used to dispose of radioactive wastewater. But environmental regulators mandated that Fluor first locate and seal a

30-year-old well, now covered over, to prevent contamination of the groundwater table. Poor historical data made it impossible to tell if the well really existed, and ground-penetrating radar also failed to discover it. Simply removing the contaminated soil to find the well would have been costly and risky for workers.

When the team posted a request to Fluor's knowledge communities, one of the experts suggested using an alternative technology from a different industry. The team tried it and found the well. In fact, within two months, Fluor went on to use the same method to locate—or prove the nonexistence of—more than 100 wells and suspected wells. Without the community's help, the project teams may have had to employ expensive, hazardous, and possibly ineffective methods. Any engineer can consult his colleagues, but Fluor's communities offer its engineers a worldwide network of expertise and connections no one person could build or maintain.

Setting Up Communities Strategically

Unlike the independent and self-organizing bodies we saw years ago, today's communities require real structure. Though we once envisioned few rules, we have since identified four principles that govern the design and integration of effective communities.

Focus on issues important to the organization

Sustainable communities tackle real problems that have been defined by senior management. At pharmaceutical firm Pfizer, one such issue is drug safety. The company has about 200 active drug development projects, all in different stages, in different countries, focusing on different disease areas, and using different processes. To advise teams on safety, two types of communities work across these projects—councils and networks. About 20% of Pfizer's safety staff are involved in one or the other.

The nine safety councils focus on major organs of the body, such as the liver or the heart, or on key issues such as pediatric safety. On average, each has a dozen members, representing individual areas of expertise, with deep knowledge of toxicology, clinical development, chemistry, and disease categories. Councils are responsible for helping development project teams make difficult judgment calls on potential safety issues. Their members can be volunteers or appointed by management. They are, as Tim Anderson, Pfizer's head of Drug Safety R&D, told us, "the most elevated form of advice-giving body on safety." Membership in a council is a major recognition of expertise.

The dozen or so networks have voluntary, open membership and focus on disciplines or practices, such as lab functions or techniques; or on emerging technologies, such as nanotechnology. When the demand for advice rises high enough, a network can be elevated to council status.

Because they cross the entire development organization, safety councils and networks can take a "portfolio" approach to potential safety issues—comparing data, tests, and results on similar compounds being developed in different therapeutic areas. Sometimes they use tests and data from one team to support decisions by another, saving months of development time. The Kidney Safety Council, for instance, suggested that new biomarker tests could help assess whether a recent safety finding in an animal model had relevance for humans, which allowed one project to move to initial clinical trials much more quickly. Because the clock on patents starts at the beginning of development, shorter development time has a significant impact on product life span and business results.

In the nonprofit world, the United Nations has established a set of 12 communities that address serious social and economic problems in India. Solution Exchange is composed of people from governmental and development agencies and nongovernmental organizations (NGOs). Addressing issues like nutrition, education, and HIV/AIDS prevention, these practitioner communities now comprise 3,000 to 4,000 members each. They enable grassroots workers to share what they've learned about implementing programs with government agencies, policy makers, and other program implementers. The members' practical insights are increasingly influencing policy design and helping create more effective programs. "We reach more people through Solution Exchange than any other program because it cuts across institutional barriers and allows people to connect regardless of source of funding, organization, or location," notes Maxine Olson, the former resident coordinator of the UN India team.

The communities also function like a research service, collecting and distilling timely suggestions for solutions to important problems. In one instance, members of the Food and Nutrition Security Community helped a midday meal program in the nation's schools by working with local growers to supply a steady stream of vegetables. In the rural south, one NGO created school kitchen gardens, where children were trained to grow vegetables on their own. The community spread these successful ideas to practitioners throughout the country. Since the typical Indian diet provides only 10% of the minimum required vitamins and minerals, the additional vegetables in school lunches led to real improvements in children's health.

Establish community goals and deliverables

Rather than inhibiting the exchange of ideas and information, formal goals and deliverables energize communities. They provide a focus—a reason to meet and participate. More important, they establish the contribution of communities to the organization.

At ConocoPhillips, communities report to functional teams, which are responsible for stewarding improvements in specific areas, such as oil and gas production. The functional teams, typically staffed by eight to 10 senior managers, have aggressive, measurable goals, like reducing the number of unrecovered barrels of oil. Each community owns part of the overall goal and tracks its progress toward achieving it. For example, when the company sought to improve the performance of its well operations globally, the functional team formed a well-optimization community, which then figured out how to reduce unplanned losses related to equipment impairment by 10% a year.

Explicit goals make communities operate more like teams on a day-to-day level, but community goals generally differ from team goals in that they're tied to long-term needs. Pfizer's safety councils assume organizationwide goals, which the project teams, with their focus on specific deliverables, could never meet. Pfizer's kidney council goals include developing a high-level, long-term strategy for research related to kidney toxicity; finding ways to share resources among kidney research projects; and evaluating external opportunities in kidney research, like strategic alliances.

Provide real governance

To be well integrated into the organization, communities, like teams, need strong, formal relationships with the organization's top leadership.

Companies often identify a senior manager to sponsor each community. This can turn out to be a dismal form of governance if those tapped for the role don't understand the purpose and value of the community and don't have the bandwidth to support its leaders. But if senior managers guide communities in a way that matches their long-term perspective, they can be very effective.

Pfizer's communities are sponsored by two senior managers, the heads of Drug Safety R&D and Safety and Risk Management, the two larger organizations the safety councils span. Both executives are highly engaged and meet semiannually with the community leaders to review goals, provide feedback, and understand the communities' impact and needs. For example, when one council proposed developing spreadsheets to mine 10 years of patient data that might reveal patterns of biomarker responses in clinical subpopulations, the sponsors suggested a more rigorous approach: creating an interactive relational database. The sponsors also ensured that the councils had the operational resources they needed, by providing them with two project managers who would help schedule meetings, track action items, maintain a website, and develop communications materials and training programs.

Set high management expectations

However intangible, management's expectations have a strong influence on communities, just as they do on teams. Senior managers' sponsorship is useless if they're not genuinely engaged with the

How Communities Differ from Teams

COMMUNITIES OF PRACTICE ARE different from teams, though less so than we originally thought. Like successful teams, successful communities have goals, deliverables, assigned leadership, accountability for results, and metrics. But they are distinct from teams in four ways:

1. **The long view.** Communities are responsible for the long-term development of a body of knowledge or discipline, even when they have annual goals. Teams, in contrast, focus on a specific deliverable.

2. **Peer collaboration and collective responsibility.** Community leaders establish the direction of the community, connect members, and facilitate discussions, but do not have authority over members.

3. **Intentional network expansion.** Professionals typically consult their peers for help with unusual or difficult technical problems. Communities deliberately seek to expand the internal and external resources and experts available to individuals.

4. **Knowledge management.** Teams typically do not have ongoing responsibility for organizing and documenting what a company has learned in a domain; rather, they focus on a given problem. Communities steward the knowledge in their domain with a view toward solving problems that have not yet been discovered.

---

communities. In India, where each Solution Exchange community is sponsored by a local UN agency office, participation dropped when engaged agency heads were replaced by less engaged ones. Communities continued to thrive only when new agency heads were committed to them.

In Schlumberger, an oil-field services provider with 77,000 employees in 80 countries, each community has a management sponsor. Most sponsors are highly engaged with their community leaders and activities. The sponsor of a geosciences community, for instance, set six challenges for it based on the division's business goals. One was to publish a series of articles about Schlumberger's research in outside journals, focusing on topics that hadn't been adequately covered in the literature—a major undertaking for the community. At Fluor, management expects communities to be *the* technical resource for the organization and create its standards and procedures. In the words of John McQuary, vice president of knowledge management, "The community leader is the highest technical authority in the company."

Maximizing Communities' Impact

Traditionally, organizations paid little attention to the operations of communities because they saw participation in them as a marginal activity, intended to benefit the members and not necessarily the company. But our research reveals that companies can increase the operational effectiveness of communities in four ways.

Set aside real time for community participation

Community leaders' biggest complaint is that they don't have enough time to execute their duties. When community leadership is a "spare time" activity, it can easily be squeezed out by more pressing priorities. Many companies have now made community leadership a formal component of job descriptions and performance appraisals. In our research we found that community leaders spend one half-day to one day a week on community management, or about 17% of their time on average. In a few organizations, community leadership is a full-time job. The UN's Solution Exchange communities each have a full-time facilitator and research associate.

Some companies link discretionary bonuses to community contributions; others make community leadership a necessary step toward promotion. At Schlumberger, part-time community leadership is one of employees' job objectives, reviewed quarterly with their managers.

Train community leaders in their role

Leading a community is different from leading a team. Communities, our research shows, provide greater value when companies systematically train their leaders. In Schlumberger's communities, leaders are elected by the members annually. New leaders take a one-day course covering the aspects of communities that are different from teams—such as understanding how to find pockets of knowledge and expertise, how to engage volunteers in activities, how to grow membership, how to work with members external to the company, and how to influence operating groups when you don't have direct authority.

ConocoPhillips requires all new community leaders to attend a boot camp that outlines what management expects from them. The training starts by spelling out how community contributions connect to business goals. Then workshops review community governance, support, and expected deliverables and what the company considers critical success factors, such as establishing goals, engaging members, and setting results metrics.

Hold face-to-face events

A decade ago many organizations thought communities were a free way to develop knowledge. All the staff had to do was participate in an occasional meeting. But today most communities of practice include employees in remote locations. While they typically use collaborative software to link remote staff, the most effective communities also hold face-to-face meetings, which usually focus on specific goals. Face-to-face contact fosters the trust and rapport members need to ask for help, admit mistakes, and learn from one another.

Schlumberger enlivens its annual community meetings with competitions for the best examples of how the company's tools improved a customer's performance. Judges are drawn from the community's field, and the criteria for winning are clearly known: technical depth, business relevance, innovativeness of approach, and overall impression. Winners of local competitions participate in regional competitions, and the winners of the regionals compete in a global competition, for which they also write a paper. Last year 36 community representatives presented ideas at this small global event of about 100 people. The winning presenters received a monetary prize and an award from the CEO and chief technology officer.

Use simple IT tools

Most communities don't need complex tools. Typically they use only a few functions, such as discussion forums, document libraries, expertise locators, on-demand teleconferencing, and online meeting spaces where members can edit documents as they discuss them. We found that simplicity, ease of use, and familiarity are far more important than functional sophistication.

When communities of practice first began to appear, we hailed them as a dirt-cheap way to distribute knowledge and share best practices. We thought they would be relatively self-organizing and self-sustaining, flying below the radar of organizational hierarchy. We thought they would flourish with little executive oversight—a notion that seemed to work well at the time. But as life and business have become more complex, we began to see that to make a difference over the long term, communities needed far more structure and oversight.

Despite this, communities remain more efficient and cheaper than other organizational resources and demand less oversight. In times when budgets have shrunk and managers are overwhelmed just dealing with the downturn, communities can be a valuable resource for coordinating work across organizational boundaries, whether across geography, as at Schlumberger and Fluor; across operating groups, as with Pfizer and ConocoPhillips; or down the value stream as at the UN in India. But communities are not as informal as was once thought, nor are they free. Though IT systems make global collaboration possible, successful communities need more. They need the human systems—focus, goals, and management attention—that integrate them into the organization. And they need to operate efficiently enough to respect experts' scarce time.

Originally published in March 2010. Reprint R1003F

Want Collaboration?

Accept—and Actively Manage—Conflict.
by Jeff Weiss and Jonathan Hughes

THE CHALLENGE IS A LONG-STANDING one for senior managers: How do you get people in your organization to work together across internal boundaries? But the question has taken on urgency in today's global and fast-changing business environment. To service multinational accounts, you increasingly need seamless collaboration across geographic boundaries. To improve customer satisfaction, you increasingly need collaboration among functions ranging from R&D to distribution. To offer solutions tailored to customers' needs, you increasingly need collaboration between product and service groups.

Meanwhile, as competitive pressures continually force companies to find ways to do more with less, few managers have the luxury of relying on their own dedicated staffs to accomplish their objectives. Instead, most must work with and through people across the organization, many of whom have different priorities, incentives, and ways of doing things.

Getting collaboration right promises tremendous benefits: a unified face to customers, faster internal decision making, reduced costs through shared resources, and the development of more innovative products. But despite the billions of dollars spent on initiatives to improve collaboration, few companies are happy with the results. Time and again we have seen management teams employ the same few strategies to boost internal cooperation. They restructure their organizations and reengineer their business processes.

They create cross-unit incentives. They offer teamwork training. While such initiatives yield the occasional success story, most of them have only limited impact in dismantling organizational silos and fostering collaboration—and many are total failures. (See the sidebar "The Three Myths of Collaboration.")

So what's the problem? Most companies respond to the challenge of improving collaboration in entirely the wrong way. They focus on the symptoms ("Sales and delivery do not work together as closely as they should") rather than on the root cause of failures in cooperation: conflict. The fact is, you can't improve collaboration until you've addressed the issue of conflict.

This can come as a surprise to even the most experienced executives, who generally don't fully appreciate the inevitability of conflict in complex organizations. And even if they do recognize this, many mistakenly assume that efforts to increase collaboration will significantly reduce that conflict, when in fact some of these efforts—for example, restructuring initiatives—actually produce more of it.

Executives underestimate not only the inevitability of conflict but also—and this is key—its importance to the organization. The disagreements sparked by differences in perspective, competencies, access to information, and strategic focus within a company actually generate much of the value that can come from collaboration across organizational boundaries. Clashes between parties are the crucibles in which creative solutions are developed and wise trade-offs among competing objectives are made. So instead of trying simply to reduce disagreements, senior executives need to embrace conflict and, just as important, institutionalize mechanisms for managing it.

Even though most people lack an innate understanding of how to deal with conflict effectively, there are a number of straightforward ways that executives can help their people—and their organizations—constructively manage it. These can be divided into two main areas: strategies for managing disagreements at the point of conflict and strategies for managing conflict upon escalation up the management chain. These methods can help a company move through the conflict that is a necessary precursor to truly effective collaboration and, more important, extract the value that often lies latent in

Idea in Brief

Companies try all kinds of ways to improve collaboration among different parts of the organization: cross-unit incentive systems, organizational restructuring, teamwork training. While these initiatives produce occasional success stories, most have only limited impact in dismantling organizational silos and fostering collaboration.

The problem? Most companies focus on the symptoms ("Sales and delivery do not work together as closely as they should") rather than on the root cause of failures in cooperation: conflict. The fact is, you can't improve collaboration until you've addressed the issue of conflict. The authors offer six strategies for effectively managing conflict:

- Devise and implement a common method for resolving conflict.

- Provide people with criteria for making trade-offs.

- Use the escalation of conflict as an opportunity for coaching.

- Establish and enforce a requirement of joint escalation.

- Ensure that managers resolve escalated conflicts directly with their counterparts.

- Make the process for escalated conflict-resolution transparent.

The first three strategies focus on the point of conflict; the second three focus on escalation of conflict up the management chain. Together they constitute a framework for effectively managing discord, one that integrates conflict resolution into day-to-day decision-making processes, thereby removing a barrier to cross-organizational collaboration.

intra-organizational differences. When companies are able to do both, conflict is transformed from a major liability into a significant asset.

Strategies for Managing Disagreements at the Point of Conflict

Conflict management works best when the parties involved in a disagreement are equipped to manage it themselves. The aim is to get people to resolve issues on their own through a process that improves—or at least does not damage—their relationships. The

The Three Myths of Collaboration

COMPANIES ATTEMPT TO FOSTER collaboration among different parts of their organizations through a variety of methods, many based on a number of seemingly sensible but ultimately misguided assumptions.

Effective Collaboration Means "Teaming"

Many companies think that teamwork training is the way to promote collaboration across an organization. So they'll get the HR department to run hundreds of managers and their subordinates through intensive two- or three-day training programs. Workshops will offer techniques for getting groups aligned around common goals, for clarifying roles and responsibilities, for operating according to a shared set of behavioral norms, and so on.

Unfortunately, such workshops are usually the right solution to the wrong problems. First, the most critical breakdowns in collaboration typically occur not on actual teams but in the rapid and unstructured interactions between different groups within the organization. For example, someone from R&D will spend weeks unsuccessfully trying to get help from manufacturing to run a few tests on a new prototype. Meanwhile, people in manufacturing begin to complain about arrogant engineers from R&D expecting them to drop everything to help with another one of R&D's pet projects. Clearly, the need for collaboration extends to areas other than a formal team.

The second problem is that breakdowns in collaboration almost always result from fundamental differences among business functions and divisions. Teamwork training offers little guidance on how to work together in the context of competing objectives and limited resources. Indeed, the frequent emphasis on common goals further stigmatizes the idea of conflict in organizations where an emphasis on "polite" behavior regularly prevents effective problem solving. People who need to collaborate more effectively usually don't need to align around and work toward a common goal. They need to quickly and creatively solve problems by managing the inevitable conflict so that it works in their favor.

An Effective Incentive System Will Ensure Collaboration

It's a tantalizing proposition: You can hardwire collaboration into your organization by rewarding collaborative behavior. Salespeople receive bonuses not only for hitting targets for their own division's products but also for hitting cross-selling targets. Staff in corporate support functions like IT and procurement have part of their bonuses determined by positive feedback from their internal clients.

Unfortunately, the results of such programs are usually disappointing. Despite greater financial incentives, for example, salespeople continue to focus on the sales of their own products to the detriment of selling integrated solutions. Employees continue to perceive the IT and procurement departments as difficult to work with, too focused on their own priorities. Why such poor results? To some extent, it's because individuals think—for the most part correctly—that if they perform well in their own operation they will be "taken care of" by their bosses. In addition, many people find that the costs of working with individuals in other parts of the organization—the extra time required, the aggravation—greatly outweigh the rewards for doing so.

Certainly, misaligned incentives can be a tremendous obstacle to cross-boundary collaboration. But even the most carefully constructed incentives won't eliminate tensions between people with competing business objectives. An incentive is too blunt an instrument to enable optimal resolution of the hundreds of different trade-offs that need to be made in a complex organization. What's more, overemphasis on incentives can create a culture in which people say, "If the company wanted me to do that, they would build it into my comp plan." Ironically, focusing on incentives as a means to encourage collaboration can end up undermining it.

Organizations Can Be Structured for Collaboration

Many managers look for structural and procedural solutions—cross-functional task forces, collaborative "groupware," complex webs of dotted reporting lines on the organization chart—to create greater internal collaboration. But bringing people together is very different from getting them to collaborate.

Consider the following scenario. Individual information technology departments have been stripped out of a company's business units and moved to a corporatewide, shared-services IT organization. Senior managers rightly recognize that this kind of change is a recipe for conflict because various groups will now essentially compete with one another for scarce IT resources. So managers try mightily to design conflict out of, and collaboration into, the new organization. For example, to enable collaborative decision making within IT and between IT and the business units, business units are required to enter requests for IT support into a computerized tracking system. The system is designed to enable managers within the IT organization to prioritize projects and optimally deploy resources to meet the various requests.

Despite painstaking process design, results are disappointing. To avoid the inevitable conflicts between business units and IT over project prioritization, managers in the business units quickly learn to bring their requests to those they know in the IT organization rather than entering the requests into the new system. Consequently, IT professionals assume that any project in the system is a lower priority—further discouraging use of the system. People's inability to deal effectively with conflict has undermined a new process specifically designed to foster organizational collaboration.

following strategies help produce decisions that are better informed and more likely to be implemented.

Devise and implement a common method for resolving conflict

Consider for a moment the hypothetical Matrix Corporation, a composite of many organizations we've worked with whose challenges will likely be familiar to managers. Over the past few years, salespeople from nearly a dozen of Matrix's product and service groups have been called on to design and sell integrated solutions to their customers. For any given sale, five or more lead salespeople and their teams have to agree on issues of resource allocation, solution design, pricing, and sales strategy. Not surprisingly, the teams are finding this difficult. Who should contribute the most resources to a particular customer's offering? Who should reduce the scope of their participation or discount their pricing to meet a customer's budget? Who should defer when disagreements arise about account strategy? Who should manage key relationships within the customer account? Indeed, given these thorny questions, Matrix is finding that a single large sale typically generates far more conflict inside the company than it does with the customer. The resulting wasted time and damaged relationships among sales teams are making it increasingly difficult to close sales.

Most companies face similar sorts of problems. And, like Matrix, they leave employees to find their own ways of resolving them. But without a structured method for dealing with these issues, people get bogged down not only in what the right result should be but also in how to arrive at it. Often, they will avoid or work around conflict, thereby forgoing important opportunities to collaborate. And when people do decide to confront their differences, they usually default to the approach they know best: debating about who's right and who's wrong or haggling over small concessions. Among the negative consequences of such approaches are suboptimal, "split-the-difference" resolutions—if not outright deadlock.

Establishing a companywide process for resolving disagreements can alter this familiar scenario. At the very least, a well-defined, well-designed conflict resolution method will reduce transaction costs, such as wasted time and the accumulation of ill will, that often come with the struggle to work though differences. At best, it will yield the innovative outcomes that are likely to emerge from discussions that draw on a multitude of objectives and perspectives. There is an array of conflict resolution methods a company can use. But to be effective, they should offer a clear, step-by-step process for parties to follow. They should also be made an integral part of existing business activities—account planning, sourcing, R&D budgeting, and the like. If conflict resolution is set up as a separate, exception-based process—a kind of organizational appeals court—it will likely wither away once initial managerial enthusiasm wanes.

At Intel, new employees learn a common method and language for decision making and conflict resolution. The company puts them through training in which they learn to use a variety of tools for handling discord. Not only does the training show that top management sees disagreements as an inevitable aspect of doing business, it also provides a common framework that expedites conflict resolution. Little time is wasted in figuring out the best way to handle a disagreement or trading accusations about "not being a team player"; guided by this clearly defined process, people can devote their time and energy to exploring and constructively evaluating a variety of options for how to move forward. Intel's systematic method for working through differences has helped sustain some of the company's hallmark qualities: innovation, operational efficiency, and the ability to make and implement hard decisions in the face of complex strategic choices.

Provide people with criteria for making trade-offs

At our hypothetical Matrix Corporation, senior managers overseeing cross-unit sales teams often admonish those teams to "do what's right for the customer." Unfortunately, this exhortation isn't much help when conflict arises. Given Matrix's ability to offer numerous combinations of products and services, company managers—each with different training and experience and access to different information, not to mention different unit priorities—have, not surprisingly, different opinions about how best to meet customers' needs.

Blue Cross and Blue Shield: build, buy, or ally?

One of the most effective ways senior managers can help resolve cross-unit conflict is by giving people the criteria for making trade-offs when the needs of different parts of the business are at odds with one another. At Blue Cross and Blue Shield of Florida, there are often conflicting perspectives over whether to build new capabilities (for example, a new claims-processing system, as in the hypothetical example below), acquire them, or gain access to them through an alliance. The company uses a grid-like poster (a simplified version of which is shown here) that helps multiple parties analyze the trade-offs associated with these three options. By checking various boxes in the grid using personalized markers, participants indicate how they assess a particular option against a variety of criteria: for example, the date by which the new capability needs to be implemented; the availability of internal resources such as capital and staff needed to develop the capability; and the degree of integration required with existing products and processes. The table format makes criteria and trade-offs easy to compare. The visual depiction of people's "votes" and the ensuing discussion help individuals see how their differences often arise from such factors as access to different data or different prioritizing of objectives. As debate unfolds—and as people move their markers in response to new information—they can see where they are aligned and where and why they separate into significant factions of disagreement. Eventually, the criteria-based dialogue tends to produce a preponderance of markers in one of the three rows, thus yielding operational consensus around a decision.

New claims-processing system

Required implementation time frame	Organizational experience level	Availability of internal resources	Volatility of environment	Complexity of solution	Availability of external resources	Required degree of integration	Required control	
>12 months	High	High	Low	Low	Low	High	High	**Build**
<6 months	Low	High to moderate	Medium	High	High	Medium	Medium	**Buy**
6–12 months	Medium	Moderate to low	High	Moderate	Moderate	Low	Low	**Ally**

Participant 1 = ✓ Participant 2 = ✓ Participant 3 = ☆ Participant 4 = ✗ Participant 5 = ✗

Source: Blue Cross and Blue Shield of Florida

Similar clashes in perspective result when exasperated senior managers tell squabbling team members to set aside their differences and "put Matrix's interests first." That's because it isn't always clear what's best for the company given the complex interplay among Matrix's objectives for revenue, profitability, market share, and long-term growth.

Even when companies equip people with a common method for resolving conflict, employees often will still need to make zero-sum trade-offs between competing priorities. That task is made much easier and less contentious when top management can clearly articulate the criteria for making such choices. Obviously, it's not easy to reduce a company's strategy to clearly defined trade-offs, but it's worth trying. For example, salespeople who know that five points of market share are more important than a ten-point increase on a customer satisfaction scale are much better equipped to make strategic concessions when the needs and priorities of different parts of the business conflict. And even when the criteria do not lead to a straightforward answer, the guidelines can at least foster productive conversations by providing an objective focus. Establishing such criteria also sends a clear signal from management that it views conflict as an inevitable result of managing a complex business.

At Blue Cross and Blue Shield of Florida, the strategic decision to rely more and more on alliances with other organizations has significantly increased the potential for disagreement in an organization long accustomed to developing capabilities in-house. Decisions about whether to build new capabilities, buy them outright, or gain access to them through alliances are natural flashpoints for conflict among internal groups. The health insurer might have tried to minimize such conflict through a structural solution, giving a particular group the authority to make decisions concerning whether, for instance, to develop a new claims-processing system in-house, to do so jointly with an alliance partner, or to license or acquire an existing system from a third party. Instead, the company established a set of criteria designed to help various groups within the organization—for example, the enterprise alliance group, IT, and marketing—to collectively make such decisions.

The criteria are embodied in a spreadsheet-type tool that guides people in assessing the trade-offs involved—say, between speed in getting a new process up and running versus ensuring its seamless integration with existing ones—when deciding whether to build, buy, or ally. People no longer debate back and forth across a table, advocating their preferred outcomes. Instead, they sit around the table and together apply a common set of trade-off criteria to the decision at hand. The resulting insights into the pros and cons of each approach enable more effective execution, no matter which path is chosen. (For a simplified version of the trade-off tool, see the exhibit "Blue Cross and Blue Shield: build, buy, or ally?")

Use the escalation of conflict as an opportunity for coaching
Managers at Matrix spend much of their time playing the organizational equivalent of hot potato. Even people who are new to the company learn within weeks that the best thing to do with cross-unit conflict is to toss it up the management chain. Immediate supervisors take a quick pass at resolving the dispute but, being busy themselves, usually pass it up to *their* supervisors. Those supervisors do the same, and before long the problem lands in the lap of a senior-level manager, who then spends much of his time resolving disagreements. Clearly, this isn't ideal. Because the senior managers are a number of steps removed from the source of the controversy, they rarely have a good understanding of the situation. Furthermore, the more time they spend resolving internal clashes, the less time they spend engaged in the business, and the more isolated they are from the very information they need to resolve the disputes dumped in their laps. Meanwhile, Matrix employees get so little opportunity to learn about how to deal with conflict that it becomes not only expedient but almost necessary for them to quickly bump conflict up the management chain.

While Matrix's story may sound extreme, we can hardly count the number of companies we've seen that operate this way. And even in the best of situations—for example, where a companywide conflict-management process is in place and where trade-off criteria are well understood—there is still a natural tendency for people to let their

IBM: coaching for conflict

Managers can reduce the repeated escalation of conflict up the management chain by helping employees learn how to resolve disputes themselves. At IBM, executives get training in conflict management and are offered online resources to help them coach others. One tool on the corporate intranet (an edited excerpt of which is shown here) walks managers through a variety of conversations they might have with a direct report who is struggling to resolve a dispute with people from one or more groups in the company—some of whom, by design, will be consulted to get their views but won't be involved in negotiating the final decision.

If you hear from someone reporting to you that . . .	The problem could be that . . .	And you could help your report by saying something like . . .
"Everyone still insists on being a decision maker."	The people your report is dealing with remain concerned that unless they have a formal voice in making the decision—or a key piece of the decision—their needs and interests won't be taken into account.	"You might want to explain why people are being consulted and how this information will be used." "Are there ways to break this decision apart into a series of sub-issues and assign decision-making roles around those subissues?" "Consider talking to the group about the costs of having everyone involved in the final decision."
"If I consult with this person up front, he might try to force an answer on me or create roadblocks to my efforts to move forward."	The person you are coaching may be overlooking the risks of not asking for input—mainly, that any decision arrived at without input could be sabotaged later on.	"How would you ask someone for input? What would you tell her about your purpose in seeking it? What questions would you ask? What would you say if she put forth a solution and resisted discussing other options?" "Is there a way to manage the risk that she will try to block your efforts other than by not consulting her at all? If you consult with her now, might that in fact lower the risk that she will try to derail your efforts later?"
"I have consulted with all the right parties and have crafted, by all accounts, a good plan. But the decision makers cannot settle on a final decision."	The right people were included in the negotiating group, but the process for negotiating a final decision was not determined.	"What are the ground rules for how decisions will be made? Do all those in the group need to agree? Must the majority agree? Or just those with the greatest competence?" "What interests underlie the objective of having everyone agree? Is there another decision-making process that would meet those interests?"

bosses sort out disputes. Senior managers contribute to this tendency by quickly resolving the problems presented to them. While this may be the fastest and easiest way to fix the problems, it encourages people to punt issues upstairs at the first sign of difficulty. Instead, managers should treat escalations as opportunities to help employees become better at resolving conflict. (For an example of how managers can help their employees improve their conflict resolution skills, see the exhibit "IBM: coaching for conflict.")

At KLA-Tencor, a major manufacturer of semiconductor production equipment, a materials executive in each division oversees a number of buyers who procure the materials and component parts for machines that the division makes. When negotiating a company-wide contract with a supplier, a buyer often must work with the company commodity manager, as well as with buyers from other divisions who deal with the same supplier. There is often conflict, for example, over the delivery terms for components supplied to two or more divisions under the contract. In such cases, the commodity manager and the division materials executive will push the division buyer to consider the needs of the other divisions, alternatives that might best address the collective needs of the different divisions, and the standards to be applied in assessing the trade-offs between alternatives. The aim is to help the buyer see solutions that haven't yet been considered and to resolve the conflict with the buyer in the other division.

Initially, this approach required more time from managers than if they had simply made the decisions themselves. But it has paid off in fewer disputes that senior managers need to resolve, speedier contract negotiation, and improved contract terms both for the company as a whole and for multiple divisions. For example, the buyers from three KLA-Tencor product divisions recently locked horns over a global contract with a key supplier. At issue was the trade-off between two variables: one, the supplier's level of liability for materials it needs to purchase in order to fulfill orders and, two, the flexibility granted the KLA-Tencor divisions in modifying the size of the orders and their required lead times. Each division demanded a different balance between these two factors, and the buyers took the conflict to their managers, wondering if they should try to negotiate each of the different trade-offs into the contract or pick among them. After being coached to consider how each division's business model shaped its preference—and using this understanding to jointly brainstorm alternatives—the buyers and commodity manager arrived at a creative solution that worked for everyone: They would request a clause in the contract that allowed them to increase and decrease flexibility in order volume and lead time, with corresponding changes in supplier liability, as required by changing market conditions.

Strategies for Managing Conflict upon Escalation

Equipped with common conflict resolution methods and trade-off criteria, and supported by systematic coaching, people are better able to resolve conflict on their own. But certain complex disputes will inevitably need to be decided by superiors. Consequently, managers must ensure that, upon escalation, conflict is resolved constructively and efficiently—and in ways that model desired behaviors.

Establish and enforce a requirement of joint escalation

Let's again consider the situation at Matrix. In a typical conflict, three salespeople from different divisions become involved in a dispute over pricing. Frustrated, one of them decides to hand the problem up to his boss, explaining the situation in a short voice-mail message. The message offers little more than bare acknowledgment of the other salespeople's viewpoints. The manager then determines, on the basis of what he knows about the situation, the solution to the problem. The salesperson, armed with his boss's decision, returns to his counterparts and shares with them the verdict—which, given the process, is simply a stronger version of the solution the salesperson had put forward in the first place. But wait! The other two salespeople have also gone to *their* managers and carried back stronger versions of *their* solutions. At this point, each salesperson is locked into what is now "my manager's view" of the right pricing scheme. The problem, already thorny, has become even more intractable.

The best way to avoid this kind of debilitating deadlock is for people to present a disagreement jointly to their boss or bosses. This will reduce or even eliminate the suspicion, surprises, and damaged personal relationships ordinarily associated with unilateral escalation. It will also guarantee that the ultimate decision maker has access to a wide array of perspectives on the conflict, its causes, and the various ways it might be resolved. Furthermore, companies that require people to share responsibility for the escalation of a conflict often see a decrease in the number of problems that are pushed up the management chain. Joint escalation helps create the kind of accountability that is lacking when people know they can provide their side of an issue to their own manager and blame others when things don't work out.

A few years ago, after a merger that resulted in a much larger and more complex organization, senior managers at the Canadian telecommunications company Telus found themselves virtually paralyzed by a daily barrage of unilateral escalations. Just determining who was dealing with what and who should be talking to whom took up huge amounts of senior management's time. So the company made joint escalation a central tenet of its new organizationwide protocols for conflict resolution—a requirement given teeth by managers' refusal to respond to unilateral escalation. When a conflict occurred among managers in different departments concerning, say, the allocation of resources among the departments, the managers were required to jointly describe the problem, what had been done so far to resolve it, and its possible solutions. Then they had to send a joint write-up of the situation to each of their bosses and stand ready to appear together and answer questions when those bosses met to work through a solution. In many cases, the requirement of systematically documenting the conflict and efforts to resolve it—because it forced people to make such efforts—led to a problem being resolved on the spot, without having to be kicked upstairs. Within weeks, this process resulted in the resolution of hundreds of issues that had been stalled for months in the newly merged organization.

Ensure that managers resolve escalated conflicts directly with *their* counterparts

Let's return to the three salespeople at Matrix who took their dispute over pricing to their respective bosses and then met again, only to find themselves further from agreement than before. So what did they do at that point? They sent the problem *back* to their bosses. These three bosses, each of whom thought he'd already resolved the issue, decided the easiest thing to do would be to escalate it themselves. This would save them time and put the conflict before senior managers with the broad view seemingly needed to make a decision. Unfortunately, by doing this, the three bosses simply perpetuated the situation their salespeople had created, putting forward a biased viewpoint and leaving it to their own managers to come up with an answer. In the end, the decision was made unilaterally by the senior manager with the most organizational clout. This result bred resentment back down the management chain. A sense of "we'll win next time" took hold, ensuring that future conflict would be even more difficult to resolve.

It's not unusual to see managers react to escalations from their employees by simply passing conflicts up their own functional or divisional chains until they reach a senior executive involved with all the affected functions or divisions. Besides providing a poor example for others in the organization, this can be disastrous for a company that needs to move quickly. To avoid wasting time, a manager somewhere along the chain might try to resolve the problem swiftly and decisively by herself. But this, too, has its costs. In a complex organization, where many issues have significant implications for numerous parts of the business, unilateral responses to unilateral escalations are a recipe for inefficiency, bad decisions, and ill feelings.

The solution to these problems is a commitment by managers—a commitment codified in a formal policy—to deal with escalated conflict directly with their counterparts. Of course, doing this can feel cumbersome, especially when an issue is time-sensitive. But resolving the problem early on is ultimately more efficient than trying to sort it out later, after a decision becomes known because it has negatively affected some part of the business.

In the 1990s, IBM's sales and delivery organization became increasingly complex as the company reintegrated previously independent divisions and reorganized itself to provide customers with full solutions of bundled products and services. Senior executives soon recognized that managers were not dealing with escalated conflicts and that relationships among them were strained because they failed to consult and coordinate around cross-unit issues. This led to the creation of a forum called the Market Growth Workshop (a name carefully chosen to send a message throughout the company that getting cross-unit conflict resolved was critical to meeting customer needs and, in turn, growing market share). These monthly conference calls brought together managers, salespeople, and frontline product specialists from across the company to discuss and resolve cross-unit conflicts that were hindering important sales—for example, the difficulty salespeople faced in getting needed technical resources from overstretched product groups.

The Market Growth Workshops weren't successful right away. In the beginning, busy senior managers, reluctant to spend time on issues that often hadn't been carefully thought through, began sending their subordinates to the meetings—which made it even more difficult to resolve the problems discussed. So the company developed a simple preparation template that forced people to document and analyze disputes before the conference calls. Senior managers, realizing the problems created by their absence, recommitted themselves to attending the meetings. Over time, as complex conflicts were resolved during these sessions and significant sales were closed, attendees began to see these meetings as an opportunity to be involved in the resolution of high-stakes, high-visibility issues.

Make the process for escalated conflict resolution transparent

When a sales conflict is resolved by a Matrix senior manager, the word comes down the management chain in the form of an action item: Put together an offering with this particular mix of products and services at these prices. The only elaboration may be an admonishment to "get the sales team together, work up a proposal, and get back to the customer as quickly as possible." The problem is solved, at least for the time being. But the salespeople—unless they have been able to divine themes from the patterns of decisions made over time—are left with little guidance on how to resolve similar issues in the future. They may justifiably wonder: How was the decision made? Based on what kinds of assumptions? With what kinds of trade-offs? How might the reasoning change if the situation were different?

In most companies, once managers have resolved a conflict, they announce the decision and move on. The resolution process and rationale behind the decision are left inside a managerial black box. While it's rarely helpful for managers to share all the gory details of their deliberations around contentious issues, failing to take the time to explain how a decision was reached and the factors that went into it squanders a major opportunity. A frank discussion of the trade-offs involved in decisions would provide guidance to people trying to resolve conflicts in the future and would help nip in the bud the kind of speculation—who won and who lost, which managers or units have the most power—that breeds mistrust, sparks turf battles, and otherwise impedes cross-organizational collaboration. In general, clear communication about the resolution of the conflict can increase people's willingness and ability to implement decisions.

During the past two years, IBM's Market Growth Workshops have evolved into a more structured approach to managing escalated conflict, known as Cross-Team Workouts. Designed to make conflict resolution more transparent, the workouts are weekly meetings of people across the organization who work together on sales and delivery issues for specific accounts. The meetings provide a public forum for resolving conflicts over account strategy, solution configuration, pricing, and delivery. Those issues that cannot be resolved at the local level are escalated to regional workout sessions attended by managers from product groups, services, sales, and finance. Attendees then communicate and explain meeting resolutions to their

reports. Issues that cannot be resolved at the regional level are escalated to an even higher-level workout meeting attended by cross-
unit executives from a larger geographic region—like the Americas
or Asia Pacific—and chaired by the general manager of the region
presenting the issue. The most complex and strategic issues reach
this global forum. The overlapping attendance at these sessions—in
which the managers who chair one level of meeting attend sessions
at the next level up, thereby observing the decision-making process
at that stage—further enhances the transparency of the system
among different levels of the company. IBM has further formalized
the process for the direct resolution of conflicts between services
and product sales on large accounts by designating a managing
director in sales and a global relationship partner in IBM global services as the ultimate point of resolution for escalated conflicts. By
explicitly making the resolution of complex conflicts part of the job
descriptions for both managing director and global relationship
partner—and by making that clear to others in the organization—
IBM has reduced ambiguity, increased transparency, and increased
the efficiency with which conflicts are resolved.

Tapping the Learning Latent in Conflict

The six strategies we have discussed constitute a framework for effectively managing organizational discord, one that integrates conflict resolution into day-to-day decision-making processes, thereby
removing a critical barrier to cross-organizational collaboration. But
the strategies also hint at something else: that conflict can be more
than a necessary antecedent to collaboration.

Let's return briefly to Matrix. More than three-quarters of all
cross-unit sales at the company trigger disputes about pricing.
Roughly half of the sales lead to clashes over account control. A substantial number of sales also produce disagreements over the design
of customer solutions, with the conflict often rooted in divisions' in-
compatible measurement systems and the concerns of some people
about the quality of the solutions being assembled. But managers

are so busy trying to resolve these almost daily disputes that they don't see the patterns or sources of conflict. Interestingly, if they ever wanted to identify patterns like these, Matrix managers might find few signs of them. That's because salespeople, who regularly hear their bosses complain about all the disagreements in the organization, have concluded that they'd better start shielding their superiors from discord.

The situation at Matrix is not unusual—most companies view conflict as an unnecessary nuisance—but that view is unfortunate. When a company begins to see conflict as a valuable resource that should be managed and exploited, it is likely to gain insight into problems that senior managers may not have known existed. Because internal friction is often caused by unaddressed strains within an organization or between an organization and its environment, setting up methods to track conflict and examine its causes can provide an interesting new perspective on a variety of issues. In the case of Matrix, taking the time to aggregate the experiences of individual salespeople involved in recurring disputes would likely lead to better approaches to setting prices, establishing incentives for salespeople, and monitoring the company's quality control process.

At Johnson & Johnson, an organization that has a highly decentralized structure, conflict is recognized as a positive aspect of cross-company collaboration. For example, a small internal group charged with facilitating sourcing collaboration among J&J's independent operating companies—particularly their outsourcing of clinical research services—actively works to extract lessons from conflicts. The group tracks and analyzes disagreements about issues such as what to outsource, whether and how to shift spending among suppliers, and what supplier capabilities to invest in. It hosts a council, comprising representatives from the various operating companies, that meets regularly to discuss these differences and explore their strategic implications. As a result, trends in clinical research outsourcing are spotted and information about them is disseminated throughout J&J more quickly. The operating companies benefit from insights about new offshoring opportunities, technologies, and ways of structuring collaboration with suppliers. And J&J, which can now piece together an accurate and global view of its suppliers, is better able to partner with them. Furthermore, the company realizes more value from its relationship with suppliers— yet another example of how the effective management of conflict can ultimately lead to fruitful collaboration.

J&J's approach is unusual but not unique. The benefits it offers provide further evidence that conflict—so often viewed as a liability to be avoided whenever possible—can be valuable to a company that knows how to manage it.

Originally published in March 2005. Reprint R0503F

Shattering the Myths About Enterprise 2.0

by Andrew P. McAfee

DIGITAL COLLABORATION IS ALL the rage in the world of business. Companies in every industry are adopting collaborative software platforms that enable employees to generate more and better output. A May 2009 Forrester Research study found that almost 50% of companies in the U.S. use some kind of social software, and a July 2009 Prescient Digital Media survey revealed that 47% of respondents were using wikis, 45% blogs, and 46% internal discussion forums.

Underpinning this trend is Web 2.0, a term coined in 2004 to describe the internet's capability to allow everyone, even non-techies, to connect with other people and contribute content. Facebook, Twitter, YouTube, and Wikipedia are the best-known examples of this trend, and they have become some of the Web's most popular resources. Three years ago, I coined the term Enterprise 2.0 to highlight the fact that smart companies are embracing Web 2.0 technologies, as well as the underlying approach to collaboration and creation of content.

Enterprise 2.0, which I sometimes call E2.0, refers to how an organization uses *emergent social software platforms,* or ESSPs, to pursue its goals (see the sidebar "What Is Enterprise 2.0?"). This definition emphasizes the most striking feature of the new technologies: They don't impose predetermined workflows, roles and responsibilities, or interdependencies among people, but instead allow them to emerge. This is a profound shift. Most companies use applications like ERP and CRM software, which create cross-functional business processes and specify—in detail and with little flexibility—exactly who does what and when, and who gets to make which decisions. E2.0, in contrast, requires companies to take the opposite approach: to let people create and refine content as equals and with no, or few, preconditions. Using ESSPs enables patterns and structures to take shape over time.

There are several benefits of ESSPs. The tools help people find information and guidance quickly—and reduce duplication of work. They open up innovation processes to more people, which is an advantage because, as open source software advocate Eric Raymond put it, "with enough eyeballs, all bugs are shallow." They harness collective intelligence and the wisdom of crowds to obtain accurate answers to tough questions. They let people build, maintain, and profit from large social networks. They allow executives to realize the dream of creating an up-to-the-minute repository of everything an organization knows. Underlying all these benefits is a style of interaction and collaboration that isn't defined by hierarchy and is relatively unconstrained by it.

However, E2.0 hasn't delivered results or even gotten off the ground everywhere. Many companies refuse to take the plunge because the possible drawbacks—the misuse of blogs or the possibility of information theft, for instance—seem concrete and immediate, whereas the benefits appear nebulous and distant. In addition, many corporations have walked away from their E2.0 initiatives, for three reasons. One, doubts persist about the value of these collaboration tools even when they are being actively used. Two, ESSPs often seem unimpressive initially. Pages in corporate wikis read like documents in a binder; blog posts look like newsletters; and personal pages look like Facebook profiles. Three, many projects simply never took off. Employees didn't flock to use the new technologies, and sponsors wound up with digital wastelands instead of the

Idea in Brief

Web 2.0 technologies are now a staple of social collaboration on the internet. In 2006 Andrew McAfee, of the MIT Center for Digital Business, coined the term Enterprise 2.0 to describe how organizations use emergent social software platforms, or ESSPs, to pursue their goals. However, some organizations don't achieve the many collaboration-related benefits that internal ESSPs can offer. After studying both successful and unsuccessful E2.0 initiatives, McAfee attributes most of the failures to five misconceptions. The first two myths crop up before an E2.0 initiative is launched. One is that the risks of ESSPs, most notably from inappropriate use, will greatly outweigh the rewards. McAfee makes the case that those dangers rarely manifest in practice. The other pre-launch myth is that the ROI of an E2.0 initiative should be calculated in monetary terms. McAfee

shows how Enterprise 2.0 can deliver valuable benefits in terms of developing human, organizational, and information capital— without a numerical ROI yield. The final three myths arise after an E2.0 project is deployed. One holds that people will flock to a collaboration platform once it is built. Success actually requires various types of top-down support, including active participation by senior leaders. Another is that E2.0's primary worth is in helping close colleagues work together better. In reality, the value extends to networks of expertise well beyond a user's inner circle. The importance of those far-reaching interpersonal connections also debunks the last myth: that E2.0 should be judged by the information it generates. Information is indeed useful, but E2.0's greatest advantage lies in transforming potential ties between people into actual ones.

rainforests they had expected. In fact, a 2008 McKinsey survey showed that only 21% of companies were entirely satisfied with their E2.0 initiatives and that 22% were entirely dissatisfied.

I have been studying E2.0 projects, both successful and unsuccessful, since companies started deploying these technologies in earnest four years ago. My research shows that, despite the failures, there have been striking successes—and that more big successes are possible if only companies would learn to use these tools well. Most initiatives fail because of five widely held beliefs: reasonable attitudes held by well-meaning people, not the handiwork of saboteurs. Nonetheless, data, research, and case studies show that the

What Is Enterprise 2.0?

ENTERPRISE 2.0 IS THE USE OF EMERGENT social software platforms, or ESSPs, by an organization to pursue its goals. Here's a breakdown of what the term means:

- *Social software,* as a Wikipedia entry roughly characterizes it, enables people to rendezvous, connect, or collaborate through computer-mediated communication and to form online communities.

- *Platforms* are digital environments in which contributions and interactions are visible to everyone and remain until the user deletes them.

- *Emergent* means that the software is "freeform" and contains mechanisms that let the patterns and structure inherent in people's interactions become evident over time.

- *Freeform* software has many or all of the following characteristics: Its use is optional; it does not predefine workflows; it is indifferent to formal hierarchies; and it accepts many types of data.

beliefs are wrong; they're the myths of Enterprise 2.0. In the following pages, I'll refute them, starting with two that crop up before an E2.0 initiative is launched and finishing with three that can take hold after deployment.

Myth 1: E2.0's Risks Greatly Outweigh the Rewards

When CEOs first hear about how Enterprise 2.0 works, many become queasy about allowing people to contribute freely to the company's content platforms. They voice a consistent set of concerns: What if someone posts hate speech or pornography? Can't an employee use the forum to denigrate the company, air dirty laundry, or criticize its leadership and strategy? Don't these technologies make it easy for valuable information to seep out of the company and be sold to the highest bidder? If we use these tools, how can we avoid breaking agreements with partners about information sharing? What if rivals use customer-facing websites to air grievances or malign our products and service? Are we liable if people give incorrect information or bad advice on the forums we host? Won't employees use the collaboration software to plan social events instead of work-related activities?

Those risks all exist in theory—but rarely in practice. Over the last four years, I've asked every company I've worked with about the worst things that have happened on their ESSPs. My collection of horror stories is nearly empty. I have yet to come across a single episode that has made me wonder whether companies shouldn't invest in E2.0 technologies. One conversation I had was particularly telling. In late 2007, when I was teaching a group of senior HR executives, one of them said that leaders at her company, which employed many young people, became concerned about how employees represented it online. When her team poked around on Facebook, MySpace, and other sites, it found that employees almost always talked about the company in appropriate ways. The worst thing the team discovered was a photograph of a training session in which some account numbers were dimly visible on a blackboard. When alerted, the employee who posted it immediately apologized and took the photograph down. Even that wasn't necessary; it turned out that the numbers were dummies.

Four factors work together to make E2.0 horror stories so rare. One, although anonymity is the default on the internet, on company intranets attribution is the norm. Users are circumspect and unlikely to "flame" colleagues. If workers do misbehave, companies can identify, counsel, educate, and, if necessary, discipline them. Two, participants usually feel a sense of community and react quickly if they feel that someone is violating the norms. Counterproductive contributions usually meet with a flurry of responses that articulate why the content is out of bounds, reiterate the implicit rules, and offer correction. Three, in addition to an organization's formal leaders, community leaders form a counterbalance. They exert a great deal of influence and shape fellow employees' behavior online. Four, the internet has been in wide use for more than a decade, so most people know how to behave appropriately in online contexts.

If corporations don't believe that these factors provide sufficient protection, they can easily set up a moderation process whereby executives vet contributions before they appear. This precaution is common on customer-facing sites, where spammers and vandals can wreak havoc, but companies can use it internally too. Don't forget, e-mail and text messages are invisible to everyone except senders and receivers, but ESSPs make content visible and thereby turn the entire workforce into compliance monitors. It's a myth that E2.0 is risky; if anything, it lowers companies' risk profiles.

Myth 2: The ROI of E2.0 Must Be Calculated in Monetary Terms

The one aspect of Enterprise 2.0 that I'm asked about more than the risks is the business case for it. E2.0 initiatives, like all IT projects, appear similar to other investment opportunities in that a company spends money to acquire assets (such as, in this case, servers and software CDs). But that's a surface-level matter; the company's deeper goal is to develop its intangible assets—notably its human, organizational, and information capital.

The value of intangible assets can't be measured independently, as several experts have noted; it stems from the assets' ability to help the organization implement its strategy. "Intangible assets, such as knowledge and technology, seldom have a direct impact on financial outcomes such as increased revenues, lowered costs, and higher profits," state HBS professor Robert Kaplan and David Norton unequivocally in their book *Strategy Maps*. Therefore, it's tough to create a business case for E2.0 projects by estimating the monetary return on investment. I have never met leaders of healthy E2.0 initiatives who wished that they had calculated an ROI figure, but I have spoken with many who described ROI exercises as a waste of time and energy.

Companies that are launching Enterprise 2.0 initiatives would do better to focus on three elements other than ROI:

- **Expected cost and timeline.** By now, managers know how to break down the cost of IT projects. They should also estimate how long the E2.0 effort will take, work out the implementation stages, and lay out the milestones.

- **Possible benefits.** The expected benefits from E2.0 must be stated, although descriptions needn't be as detailed as those for the features of a piece of software or as grandiose as the

Enterprise 2.0's Benefits

HERE ARE SIX BENEFITS A COMPANY can get by deploying and using an emergent social software platform:

1. **Group editing** allows multiple people to collaborate on a centrally stored work product such as a document, spreadsheet, presentation, or website.

2. **Authoring** is the ability to generate content and to publish it online for a broad audience. Unlike sending e-mail, authoring is a public act.

3. **Broadcast search** refers to the posting of queries in a public forum in the hope of receiving an answer. People publicize not what they know, but what they don't know.

4. **Network formation and maintenance.** Social network applications keep people in touch with the activities of close and distant contacts. Whenever a user provides an update, it becomes available to the entire network.

5. **Collective intelligence** is the use of technologies, such as prediction markets, to generate answers and forecasts from a dispersed group.

6. **Self-organization** is the ability of users to build communities and information resources without explicit coordination by any central authority. This is the most remarkable benefit of Enterprise 2.0—and the easiest to overlook.

---

promised results from ERP and CRM implementations such as "organizational transformation" or "customer intimacy." (See the sidebar "Enterprise 2.0's Benefits.")

- **Expected footprint.** Managers should detail the geographic, divisional, and functional reach of the E2.0 projects they are planning.

These three parameters are usually sufficient to allow executives to make decisions about whether it's worth investing in E2.0 projects. Most have little trouble answering questions such as "Is it worth spending $50,000 over the next six months to build a broadcast search system for the company?" The answer won't be an ROI number, but managers can nonetheless address it adeptly. Walking away from the classic business case doesn't mean abandoning clear thinking or planning. However, it's time to replace the myth that E2.0 requires an ROI calculation with the fact that tangible assets can deliver intangible benefits.

Myth 3: If We Build It, They Will Come

Given the popularity of Wikipedia, Facebook, and Twitter, many executives assume that their companies' collaboration platforms will also attract masses of people. They adopt a passive rollout strategy, introduce a few ESSPs, and formally notify people that the forums exist. They then wait for the benefits to accrue—and are shocked when nothing happens.

Popular as large Web 2.0 communities like Facebook are, they still attract only a tiny percentage of internet users. The main task that E2.0 champions face is to draw in a greater fraction of their target audience. That's difficult for two reasons. One, people are busy. Few knowledge workers feel they have the time to take on an additional responsibility, especially one with ill-defined goals and expectations. Two, employees don't know how top management will view their participation in ESSPs. Will senior executives value employees who contribute, or will they assume that those workers aren't interested in their "real" jobs? When the answer isn't clear, an unfortunate sequence of events unfolds. A few people start using the new tools out of curiosity or enthusiasm. They soon perceive that they're talking only to each other or, worse, to no one. Shouting into a void loses its appeal quickly, so they stop. The project is then considered a failure.

To avoid this outcome, I advocate the use of explicit recognition programs, incentives, and other types of top-down support for E2.0 projects. That's how the formal organization can show that it values employees' contributions. Leaders also should use ESSPs themselves. When senior executives allow their blog posts to receive comments and then respond to the feedback, or use social networking software to create a profile and connect with others in the organization, they're demonstrating their belief in E2.0. Similarly, when a company recognizes those who answer others' questions, it asserts that this type of work is valid and valuable. That E2.0 will automatically lure people is a myth; only when people know they're being heard by those who matter will E2.0 become mainstream.

Myth 4: E2.0 Delivers Value Mainly by Helping Close Colleagues Work Better

Most companies currently use ESSPs to support people who are already collaborating. The Prescient Digital Media survey cited earlier, for example, found that E2.0's most popular uses are employee collaboration (77% of respondents) and knowledge management (71%). When those are the goals, a typical scenario is for the organization to establish group-editing environments for all the units—such as labs, workgroups, business units, client teams, and so on—that want them, or to let the entities set them up for themselves. In most cases, these environments are closed: Nobody outside the predefined group can see or edit the content.

However, this approach has shortcomings. Consider the types of interpersonal ties of a typical knowledge worker. She has a small group of close collaborators with whom she has strong professional relationships. There's also a large set of people to whom she has weak ties: coworkers she interacts with periodically, colleagues she knows through coworkers, and other professional acquaintances. Next is another, even larger set of employees who may be valuable to her if only she knew about them. They could keep her from reinventing the wheel on her next project, answer pressing questions, tell her about a good vendor or consultant, let her know that they're working on similar problems, and so on. Finally are the people who wouldn't become colleagues of the knowledge worker even if she had ties to them.

Picture a bull's-eye with four rings; it can represent these four kinds of ties. When an E2.0 initiative consists of closed editing environments, it ignores the benefits that the three outer rings can deliver. Network formation often happens in the second ring. Authoring and broadcast search convert potential ties into actual ones, so they extend to people in the third ring. And collective intelligence works across all four rings; even strangers can trade with one another in prediction markets and generate accurate forecasts.

In short, the benefits of E2.0 technologies manifest themselves in all four rings. It's a myth that companies should focus on group editing among close colleagues; the reality is that Enterprise 2.0 is valuable at every level of interpersonal ties.

Myth 5: E2.0 Should Be Judged by the Information It Generates

It's commonly believed that the value of E2.0 can be assessed by looking at the information it yields. Popular Web 2.0 resources reinforce this idea: Wikipedia is a huge collection of articles, Flickr of pictures, and del.icio.us of web bookmarks. All of them deliver value to users mainly because they're comprehensive and of reasonable quality. It seems logical, then, to judge an organization's collaborative software platforms with one eye on quality and the other on comprehensiveness. This isn't unfair, but it is incomplete. First, ESSPs often capture work in progress rather than polished deliverables. Wiki pages and blog posts will look rough because they're essentially drafts. They're meant to present raw ideas—not refined ones. People should be encouraged to air first-cut concepts in order to show what they're planning to work on, what they're interested in, and what they know. Second, content points to people. Imperfect or incomplete information is valuable when organizations can identify who posted it. The social connection is often the real benefit that E2.0 delivers.

In 2008, for example, Don Burke, one of the evangelists for the U.S. intelligence community's Intellipedia wiki, posted some questions on my behalf on his internal blog. The first was "What, if anything, do Enterprise 2.0 tools let you do that you simply couldn't do before? In other words, have these tools incrementally changed your ability to do your job, or have they more fundamentally changed what your job is and how you do it?" Most respondents stressed the value of the platform's ability to convert potential ties into actual ones. Here are comments from a few of them:

- **From a Defense Intelligence Agency analyst:** "These tools have immensely improved my ability to interact with people that I would never have met otherwise . . . People that would never have been visible before now have a voice."

- **From a National Security Agency analyst:** "Earlier, contacting other agencies was done cautiously and only through official channels. After nearly two years of Intellipedia, this has changed. Using it has become part of my work process, and I have made connections with a variety of analysts outside the intelligence community. I don't know everything, but I do know who I can go to when I need to find out something."

- **From a National Security Agency engineer:** "There's now a place I can go to for answers as opposed to data. By using that data and all the links to people associated with that data, I can find people who are interested in helping me understand the subject matter . . . Their helpful attitude makes me want to help them (and others) in return."

- **From a Central Intelligence Agency analyst:** "The first aspect that comes to mind is the ease of sharing ideas and working collaboratively with intelligence professionals around the world . . . I am actively involved in an early-stage project that would be impossible without these tools."

These responses may not represent the views of the entire intelligence community, but they clearly illustrate that Enterprise 2.0 lets people find new colleagues by converting potential ties into actual ties. The new connections result from content posted on platforms but are invisible in the content itself. E2.0 doesn't only generate information; that's a myth. It also helps connect people.

Nelson Mandela wrote in his autobiography about a leadership lesson he learned from a tribal chief in South Africa: "A leader . . . is like a shepherd. He stays behind the flock, letting the most nimble go out ahead, whereupon the others follow, not realizing that all along they are being directed from behind." Similarly, E2.0 reveals the domains in which people are adept, allows some to show the way, and gets others

How Smart Companies Use Enterprise 2.0

ENTERPRISE 2.0, WHEN IT WORKS, delivers impressive results, as these four examples show:

- Office supply company VistaPrint started a wiki in order to capture what a new engineering hire needed to know. Because this knowledge base often changed quickly, the company suspected that a paper-based solution would become obsolete. Within 18 months, the wiki grew to over 11,000 pages and 600 categories, all generated by employees rather than by a knowledge-management staff.

- Serena Software encouraged its employees to create profiles on Facebook and other social networking sites, both to learn more about one another and to interact with outside parties such as customers and prospective employees. The company eventually attracted twice as many people to its annual user conference—and much better candidates for its job openings.

- The U.S. government has deployed ESSPs across its 16 intelligence agencies, which include the CIA, FBI, National Security Agency, and Defense Intelligence Agency. An internal report concluded that these tools, which include blogs and the Intellipedia wiki, are "already impacting the work practices of analysts. In addition, [they are] challenging deeply held norms about controlling the flow of information between individuals and across organizational boundaries."

- A U.S. gaming company set up an internal prediction market to forecast the sales of a new product. Consumer enthusiasm for new titles is notoriously hard to predict, but the market provided a good crystal ball. The 1,200 employees who traded in the market collectively generated a forecast that turned out to be 61% more accurate than the initial prediction, which had been yielded by conventional means.

to follow them when it's in the company's best interest. Enlightened business leaders will use these technologies to lead from behind; the rest will be held back by the fears that stem from believing in myths.

Originally published in November 2009. Reprint W0911A

When Internal Collaboration Is Bad for Your Company

by Morten T. Hansen

INTERNAL COLLABORATION IS ALMOST universally viewed as good for an organization. Leaders routinely challenge employees to tear down silos, transcend boundaries, and work together in cross-unit teams. And although such initiatives often meet with resistance because they place an extra burden on individuals, the potential benefits of collaboration are significant: innovative cross-unit product development, increased sales through cross-selling, the transfer of best practices that reduce costs.

But the conventional wisdom rests on the false assumption that the more employees collaborate, the better off the company will be. In fact, collaboration can just as easily undermine performance. I've seen it happen many times during my 15 years of research in this area. In one instance, Martine Haas, of Wharton, and I studied more than 100 experienced sales teams at a large information technology consulting firm. Facing fierce competition from such rivals as IBM and Accenture for contracts that might be worth $50 million or more, teams putting together sales proposals would often seek advice from other teams with expertise in, say, a technology being implemented by the prospective client. Our research yielded a surprising conclusion about this seemingly sensible practice: The greater the collaboration (measured by hours of help a team received), the worse the result (measured by success in winning contracts). We ultimately determined that experienced teams typically didn't learn as much from their peers as they thought they did. And whatever marginal knowledge they did gain was often outweighed by the time taken away from their work on the proposal.

The problem here wasn't collaboration per se; our statistical analysis found that novice teams at the firm actually benefited from exchanging ideas with their peers. Rather, the problem was determining when it makes sense and, crucially, when it doesn't. Too often a business leader asks, How can we get people to collaborate more? That's the wrong question. It should be, Will collaboration on this project create or destroy value? In fact, to collaborate well is to know when not to do it.

This article offers a simple calculus for differentiating between "good" and "bad" collaboration using the concept of a collaboration premium. My aim is to ensure that groups in your organization are encouraged to work together only when doing so will produce better results than if they worked independently.

How Collaboration Can Go Wrong

In 1996 the British government warned that so-called mad cow disease could be transferred to humans through the consumption of beef. The ensuing panic and disastrous impact on the worldwide beef industry over the next few years drove food companies of all kinds to think about their own vulnerability to unforeseen risks.

The Norwegian risk-management services firm Det Norske Veritas, or DNV, seemed well positioned to take advantage of the business opportunity this represented by helping food companies improve food safety. Founded in 1864 to verify the safety of ships, DNV had expanded over the years to provide an array of risk-management services through some 300 offices in 100 countries.

In the fall of 2002 DNV began to develop a service that would combine the expertise, resources, and customer bases of two of the

Idea in Brief

Are you promoting cross-unit collaboration for collaboration's sake? If so, you may be putting your company at risk. Collaboration can deliver tremendous benefits (innovative offerings, new sales). But it can also backfire if its costs (including delays stemming from turf battles) prove larger than you expected.

To distinguish good collaboration from bad, estimate three factors:

- **Return:** "What cash flow would this collaboration generate if executed effectively?"

- **Opportunity cost:** "What cash flow would we pass up by investing in this project instead of a noncollaborative one?"

- **Collaboration costs:** "What cash flow would we lose owing to problems associated with cross-unit work?"

Would the return exceed the combined opportunity and collaboration costs? If yes, put that collaborative project in motion.

firm's business units: standards certification and risk-management consulting. The certification business had recently created a practice that inspected large food company production chains. The consulting business had also targeted the food industry as a growth area, with the aim of helping companies reduce risks in their supply chains and production processes.

Initial projections for a joint effort were promising: If the two businesses collaborated, cross-marketing their services to customers, they could realize 200% growth from 2004 to 2008, as opposed to 50% if they operated separately. The net cash flow projected for 2004 through 2008 from the joint effort was $40 million. (This and other DNV financial figures are altered here for reasons of confidentiality.)

The initiative was launched in 2003 and run by a cross-unit team charged with cross-selling the two types of services and developing new client relationships with food companies. But the team had trouble capitalizing on what looked like a golden opportunity. Individual business unit revenue from areas where the existing businesses had been strong—Norway for consulting services, for example, and Italy

Idea in Practice

In deciding whether to launch a collaborative effort, managers can fall victim to three common errors. By understanding these errors, you stand a better chance of avoiding them.

Overestimating the Return

Many companies place a mistakenly high economic value on collaboration. Often, the expected results don't materialize.

> **Example:** Daimler's $36 billion acquisition of Chrysler in 1998 failed to deliver the promised synergies between the two automakers. In 2007, Daimler sold 80% of Chrysler for a mere $1 billion.

Ignoring Opportunity Costs

Executives often fail to consider opportunities they would forgo by devoting resources to a particular collaborative project. They don't evaluate *non*collaborative activities that might have higher potential.

> **Example:** Risk-management services firm DNV decided to combine the expertise, resources, and customer bases of two business units—standards certification and risk-management consulting. The goal? To cross-sell services to help food companies improve food safety. DNV estimated the collaboration's return as $40 million.

But DNV never compared the food-industry opportunity that required cross-unit collaboration with other industry opportunities that wouldn't require collaboration. One opportunity in IT could have been pursued by the

for certification—continued to grow, exceeding projections in 2004. But the two units did little cross-pollination in those markets. Furthermore, the team couldn't get much traction in the United Kingdom and other targeted markets, which was particularly disappointing given that the certification group had established good relations with UK food regulators in the years following the outbreak of mad cow disease.

As new business failed to materialize, the consulting group, which was under pressure from headquarters to improve its overall results in the near term, began shifting its focus from the food industry to other sectors it had earlier targeted for growth, weakening the joint effort. The certification group continued to make the consulting unit alone, and it had more potential than the food opportunity. But because many of the consulting unit's experts were tied up with the food initiative, progress on the IT opportunity was constrained. The cost of the forgone opportunity was $25 million in revenue.

Underestimating Collaboration Costs

In most companies, it's difficult to get people in different units to work together effectively because:

- People don't want to share resources or customers.

- They resent taking on extra work if it provides little recognition and no financial incentive.

- They have conflicting priorities; for example, some people are dedicated to the initiative full-time, while others aren't.

These tensions create problems that, combined with opportunity costs, can eat into the collaboration's potential—and produce a collaboration *penalty*.

Example: At DNV, competition over customers between the two units caused tensions that ultimately scotched 50% of cross-selling engagements. That amounted to $20 million in collaboration costs. Added to the $25 million opportunity cost for the noncollaborative IT opportunity, total costs were $45 million—$5 million *over* the collaborative food opportunity's expected return of $40 million.

food industry a priority, but with the two groups' combined food industry revenue lagging behind projections in 2005, DNV abandoned the initiative it had launched with such optimism only two years before.

Knowing When (and When Not) to Collaborate

DNV's experience is hardly atypical. All too often plans involving collaboration among different parts of an organization are unveiled with fanfare only to collapse or fizzle out later. The best way to avoid such an outcome is to determine *before* you launch an initiative whether it is likely to yield a *collaboration premium*.

A collaboration premium is the difference between the projected financial return on a project and two often overlooked factors—opportunity cost and collaboration costs. In simple form:

Projected – Opportunity

cost – Collaboration costs
Collaboration premium

The projected return on a project is the cash flow it is expected to generate. The opportunity cost is the cash flow an organization passes up by devoting time, effort, and resources to the collaboration project instead of to something else—particularly something that doesn't require collaboration. Collaboration costs are those arising from the challenges involved in working across organizational boundaries—across business units, functional groups, sales offices, country subsidiaries, manufacturing sites. Cross-company collaboration typically means traveling more, coordinating work, and haggling over objectives and the sharing of information. The resulting tension that can develop between parties often creates significant costs: delays in getting to market, budget overruns, lower quality, limited cost savings, lost sales, damaged customer relationships.

Including collaboration costs makes this analysis different from the usual go/no-go decision making for proposed projects. Obviously, such costs can't be precisely quantified, especially before a project is under way. Still, with some work you can arrive at good approximations. Given how much time managers already spend estimating the return on a project—and, occasionally, the associated opportunity cost—it makes sense to take the additional step of estimating collaboration costs, particularly because they can doom a project.

If, after going through this exercise, you don't foresee a collaboration premium—or if a collaboration *penalty* is likely—the project shouldn't be approved. Indeed, this sort of analysis might have helped DNV steer clear of a promising but ultimately costly business venture.

Avoiding Collaboration That Destroys Value

In calculating the collaboration premium, it's important to avoid several common errors.

Don't overestimate the financial return

Whether because of enthusiasm for collaboration or the natural optimism of managers, many companies place a mistakenly high value on collaboration. Especially when a team's work appears to be a model of collaboration—the parties freely share resources and cooperate in resolving differences while coming up with nifty ideas—it may be easy to overlook the fact that the work is actually generating little value for the company. Never forget that the goal of collaboration is not collaboration but, rather, business results that would be impossible without it.

In numerous well-known instances, collaboration premiums failed to materialize. Daimler's $36 billion acquisition of Chrysler in 1998—with its promise of synergies between the two automakers—and the sale nine years later of 80% of Chrysler for a pitiful $1 billion constitute only the most conspicuous recent example. But collaboration's benefits are usually overvalued in much more mundane settings. Recall how the experienced sales teams at the IT consulting firm that Martine Haas and I studied shared expertise as a matter of course during the preparation of project proposals—never stopping to seriously consider whether they in fact benefited from doing so.

Don't ignore opportunity costs

Executives evaluating any proposed business project should take into account the opportunities they will forgo by devoting resources to that project. If the project requires collaboration, it's important to consider alternative noncollaborative activities with potentially higher returns. The opportunity cost is the estimated cash flow from the most attractive project *not* undertaken.

DNV didn't overestimate the potential financial return of its food initiative, but it did fail to assess the opportunity cost. "There was no consensus at the top level that food was interesting or a priority," said one senior manager. "We had not evaluated the food opportunity against other industry segments." In fact, food was only one of several sectors—including information technology, health care, and government—that DNV's consulting unit had targeted in 2001 as offering growth potential for its risk-management services. The opportunity in IT, which the consulting unit could have pursued on its own, undoubtedly had more potential. The unit made progress in 2004 generating new business in this sector, but it was constrained by a shortage of qualified consultants, some of whom were tied up with the food initiative. To pursue the food initiative, the consulting unit had to forgo additional business from the IT opportunity. I estimate the cost of this forgone opportunity at $25 million or more in lost cash flow.

Don't underestimate collaboration costs

In most companies it's difficult to get people in different units to work together effectively. Issues relating to turf, such as the sharing of resources and customers, often make groups resistant to collaboration. Individuals may resent taking on extra work if they don't get additional recognition or financial incentives. Even when collaboration delivers obvious and immediate benefits to those involved (for example, one unit's software package solves another's current problem), blending the work of two units that usually operate independently creates impediments.

These costs, which should be assessed before committing to a cross-unit project, can be tough to identify and quantify. And they will vary depending on the collaboration culture of an organization. But although they can be reduced over time through companywide efforts to foster collaboration, it's a mistake to underestimate them in the hope that collaboration can be mandated or will naturally improve during the course of a project.

As DNV decided whether to move forward with its food initiative, the project managers failed to consider the substantial collaboration costs the company would incur because it wasn't set up to collaborate. Mistrust between the consulting and certification units

Collaboration During a Recession

INTERNAL COLLABORATION, OFTEN INTENDED to spur new product development or increase revenue, may seem a low priority in a period of profit-focused cost cutting. That's a big mistake. Collaboration ought to be a crucial element of your recession strategy, because it will allow you to generate profits by exploiting existing assets—to do more with what you already have.

Wells Fargo headed into the 2002 recession with an enviable record of cross-selling 3.8 products, on average, per household customer. In 2002 the bank increased this number to an astonishing 4.2—that is, it sold nearly one additional financial product for every two customers in the middle of a recession, squeezing additional profits out of its existing customer base.

Three kinds of collaboration are especially valuable in a recession:

Cross-Selling
Follow the example of Wells Fargo and start programs to sell additional products to existing customers, who are more likely than those who don't know you to buy from you. This can increase your sales and lower the cost of selling, thus raising your profit per customer.

Best-Practice Transfer
Identify units in your company that are particularly efficient at certain activities—for example, the sales office with the lowest personnel costs—and get other units to follow their example. This can improve productivity and lower costs per employee.

Cross-Unit Product Innovation
Find ways of combining existing technologies, products, and brands to create new products, and brands to create new products and services. This is cheaper than developing them from scratch and more likely to succeed because you draw on tested intellectual property. It can increase the number of new products, speed them to market, and lower development costs.

---

escalated as they tried—unsuccessfully, and with much quarreling—to build a common customer database. "All the team members tried to protect their own customers," one manager in the certification group admitted. Because of the reluctance to share customer relationships, the team had to significantly reduce its estimates of the revenue to be generated by cross-selling.

Individual members of the cross-unit team were also pulled by conflicting goals and incentives. Only one team member was dedicated to the initiative full-time; most people had to meet individual targets within their respective units while also working on the joint project. Some people got a dressing down from their managers if their cross-unit work didn't maximize their own unit's revenue.

Even those who saw the benefits of the initiative found it hard to balance their two roles. "We all had personal agendas," said one senior manager in the certification group. "It was difficult to prioritize the food initiative and to pull people out of their daily work to do the cross-area work."

Although assigning a financial number to collaboration costs is difficult, I estimate that the cash flow sacrificed as a result of tension between the two groups, which scotched probably one in two cross-selling opportunities, was roughly $20 million.

Had the likely opportunity and collaboration costs of DNV's food-safety project been estimated, the project would have looked decidedly less attractive. In fact, managers would have seen that, rather than a collaboration premium, it was likely to yield a collaboration penalty of something like $5 million—that is, the projected return of $40 million less an opportunity cost of $25 million and collaboration costs of $20 million.

How Collaboration Can Go Right

That's not the end of DNV's story, however. Several months after the firm abandoned the food-safety initiative, Henrik Madsen was named CEO. He had seen firsthand the poor business results, wasted management effort, and ill will spawned by the initiative, having been head of the certification unit at the time. But he also believed that performance could be enhanced by collaboration at the traditionally decentralized DNV.

Madsen quickly reorganized the firm into four market-oriented business units and began looking for collaboration opportunities. His executive committee systematically evaluated all the possible pairings of units and identified a number of promising opportunities for cross-selling. The unit-by-unit analysis also revealed something else important: pairings that offered no real opportunities for collaboration—an insight that would prevent wasted efforts in the future.

The disciplined process prompted the committee to assess the potential financial return of each opportunity. Estimates totaled roughly 10% of the company's revenue at the time. The projected returns helped the committee prioritize options and assess the opportunity cost of choosing one over another. On the basis of these findings, along with an assessment of likely collaboration costs, the company launched a round of collaboration initiatives.

One of these involved the maritime unit, which provides detailed classification of vessels for companies in the shipping industry, and the IT unit, which specializes in risk-management services for IT systems in many industries. Because ships today operate using sophisticated computer systems, someone needs to help shipping companies manage the risk that those systems will malfunction at sea. There was a clear opportunity to sell IT's services to the maritime unit's customers—if effective collaboration could be achieved between the two units. That opportunity has already borne fruit: The IT unit won a contract to develop information systems for a huge cruise ship being built by a longtime customer of the maritime unit.

The IT unit has also collaborated with the company's energy business to jointly sell services to oil and drilling companies—another opportunity identified in the executive committee's review. That effort enhances the IT unit's service offering with the energy unit's oil and gas industry expertise, a package that most IT competitors can't match. The two units split the revenue, which creates incentives for both.

In pursuing opportunities like these, DNV has worked to reduce some of the typical costs of collaboration. Annie Combelles, the chief operating officer of the IT business, says there was an obvious market for her unit's services among customers of the maritime and energy units. "My concern was that those units understand what we could deliver," she says. "My concern was internal, not external." The IT group appointed a business development manager who had worked at DNV for 12 years, including a stint in the maritime unit, and had a broad personal network within the company. This made him a trusted and knowledgeable liaison to the maritime and other units, reducing potential conflict between them and the IT unit.

What's more, the IT unit has moved cautiously in trying to capitalize on opportunities for internal collaboration. Although the maritime group's longtime relationship with the cruise ship operator provided entrée for the information technology group, maritime didn't want any missteps from IT to jeopardize that valuable relationship. IT therefore initially proposed a risk-assessment project in nonvital areas of the ship such as the "hotel" function, which included the Wi-Fi network, gambling computers, and the 5,000 personal computers to be used by guests. It evaluated each of these systems and identified 30 risks. This success led to a project involving vital areas of the ship, such as the power-management and positioning systems.

DNV's renewed effort to encourage cross-unit collaboration is a work in progress that has nonetheless already produced some hard results: The portion of the IT unit's sales that came from cross-unit collaboration climbed from almost nothing to 5% in 2008, and is projected to be 10% in 2009 and 30% the following year.

Business leaders who trumpet the benefits of working together for the good of the organization are right in seeing collaboration's tremendous potential. But they should temper those exhortations with the kind of analysis I've described here, which provides needed discipline in deciding when collaboration creates—or destroys— value. Ideally, as organizations become better at collaboration, through incentives and shifts in corporate culture, the associated costs will fall and the percentage of projects likely to benefit will rise.

Although the collaboration imperative is a hallmark of today's business environment, the challenge is not to cultivate more collaboration. Rather, it's to cultivate the right collaboration, so that we can achieve the great things not possible when we work alone.

Originally published in April 2009. Reprint R0904G

Which Kind of Collaboration Is Right for You?

by Gary P. Pisano and Roberto Verganti

IN AN ERA WHEN great ideas can sprout from any corner of the world and IT has dramatically reduced the cost of accessing them, it's now conventional wisdom that virtually no company should innovate on its own. The good news is that potential partners and ways to collaborate with them have both expanded enormously in number. The bad news is that greater choice has made the perennial management challenge of selecting the best options much more difficult. Should you open up and share your intellectual property with the community? Should you nurture collaborative relationships with a few carefully selected partners? Should you harness the "wisdom of crowds"? The fervor around open models of collaboration such as crowdsourcing notwithstanding, there is no best approach to leveraging the power of outsiders. Different modes of collaboration involve different strategic trade-offs. Companies that choose the wrong mode risk falling behind in the relentless race to develop new technologies, designs, products, and services.

All too often firms jump into relationships without considering their structure and organizing principles—what we call the *collaborative architecture*. To help senior managers make better decisions about the kinds of collaboration their companies adopt, we have developed a relatively simple framework. The product of our 20 years of research and consulting in this area, it focuses on two basic questions: Given your strategy, how open or closed should your firm's network of collaborators be? And who should decide which problems the network will tackle and which solutions will be adopted?

Collaboration networks differ significantly in the degree to which membership is open to anyone who wants to join. In totally open collaboration, or crowdsourcing, everyone (suppliers, customers, designers, research institutions, inventors, students, hobbyists, and even competitors) can participate. A sponsor makes a problem public and then essentially seeks support from an unlimited number of problem solvers, who may contribute if *they* believe they have capabilities and assets to offer. Open-source software projects such as Linux, Apache, and Mozilla are examples of these networks. Closed networks, in contrast, are like private clubs. Here, you tackle the problem with one or more parties that *you* select because you deem them to have capabilities and assets crucial to the sought-after innovation.

Collaboration networks also differ fundamentally in their form of governance. In some the power to decide which problems are most important, how they'll be solved, what constitutes an acceptable solution, and which solutions should be implemented is completely vested in one firm in the network: the "kingpin." Such networks are hierarchical. Other networks are flat: The players are equal partners in the process and share the power to decide key issues.

Discussions of collaborative innovation in both academic journals and the popular media often wrongly link "openness" only with "flatness"—and even suggest that open, flat approaches are always superior. The notion is deeply flawed, however.

As the exhibit "The four ways to collaborate" shows, there are four basic modes of collaboration: a closed and hierarchical network (an *elite circle*), an open and hierarchical network (an *innovation mall*), an open and flat network (an *innovation community*), and a closed and flat network (a *consortium*).

Idea in Brief

As potential innovation partners and ways to collaborate with them proliferate, it's tough deciding how best to leverage outsiders' power.

To select the right type of collaboration options for your business, Pisano and Verganti recommend understanding the four basic collaboration modes. These modes differ along two dimensions: *openness* (can anyone participate, or just select players?) and *hierarchy* (who makes key decisions—one "kingpin" participant or all players?).

- In the *open, hierarchical* mode, anyone can offer ideas but your company defines the problem and chooses the solution.

- In the *open, flat* mode, anyone can solicit and offer ideas, and no single participant has the authority to decide what is or isn't a valid innovation.

- In the *closed, hierarchical* mode, your company selects certain participants and decides which ideas get developed.

- In the *closed, flat* mode, a select group is invited to offer ideas. But participants share information and intellectual property and make critical decisions together.

Each mode has trade-offs. For example, open networks (whether hierarchical or flat) produce many ideas, but screening them is costly. What to do? Choose modes best suited to your capabilities. For instance, if you can evaluate ideas cheaply but no single participant has all the necessary expertise to shape the innovation, use an open, flat collaboration.

When figuring out which mode is most appropriate for a given innovation initiative, a firm should consider the trade-offs of each, weighing the modes' advantages against the associated challenges and assessing the organizational capabilities, structure, and assets required to manage those challenges. (See the exhibit "How to choose the best mode of collaboration.") Its executives should then choose the mode that best suits the firm's strategy.

Open or Closed Network?

The costs of searching for, screening, and selecting contributors grow as the network becomes larger and can become prohibitive. So understanding when you need a small or a large number of problem

Idea in Practice

Understanding Your Collaboration Options

Dimension	Advantages	Challenges	When to use
Open	• You attract a wide range of possible ideas from domains beyond your experience.	• Screening all the ideas is time-consuming and expensive. • The best idea generators prefer closed networks, where their ideas are more likely implemented.	• You can evaluate proposed solutions cheaply. • You don't know what users want.
Closed	• You receive the best solution from a select knowledge domain.	• You have to know how to identify the right knowledge domain and pick the right parties.	• You need a small number of problem solvers. • You know the correct knowledge domain and parties to draw on.
Hierarchical	• Kingpins control the direction and value of the innovation.	• The right direction may be unclear.	• You have the capabilities and knowledge needed to define the problem and evaluate proposed solutions.
Flat	• Players share the costs, risks, and technical challenges of innovating.	• All parties must arrive at mutually beneficial solutions.	• No single player in the network has the necessary breadth of perspective or capabilities to solve the innovation problem.

Examples of Collaboration Options

Mode	Example
Open, hierarchical	Through InnoCentive.com, sponsor companies post scientific problems that are smaller pieces of their larger R&D program. Anyone can offer solution ideas. The "kingpins" understand the relevant technologies and user needs and can coordinate collaborators' work.
Open, flat	In open-source software community Linux, anyone can participate, define valid innovations, and use any code they deem useful.
Closed, hierarchical	Home-products design company Alessi draws on the talents of 200 independent designers. It decides who participates in its network, which concepts get developed, and which products are launched.
Closed, flat	IBM invited a few select partners to join its Microelectronics Joint Development Alliance for developing semiconductor technologies such as memory and chip-manufacturing processes. Each member has a voice in how technologies are developed.

Choosing Your Collaboration Approach

Select the collaboration mode that best suits your capabilities and strategy.

Example: In developing the iPhone and its applications, Apple initially used closed, hierarchical networks, where it could better control components influencing users' experiences. But once the iPhone was established, Apple defined a growth strategy hinging on adding software functionality and applications. Because it knew it couldn't anticipate all the applications iPhone users might value, it switched to an open, flat network: It introduced a kit allowing third-party developers to create applications based on the iPhone OS platform and to provide them to users directly through the device.

The four ways to collaborate

There are two basic issues that executives should consider when deciding how to collaborate on a given innovation project: Should membership in a network be open or closed? And, should the network's governance structure for selecting problems and solutions be flat or hierarchical? This framework reveals four basic modes of collaboration.

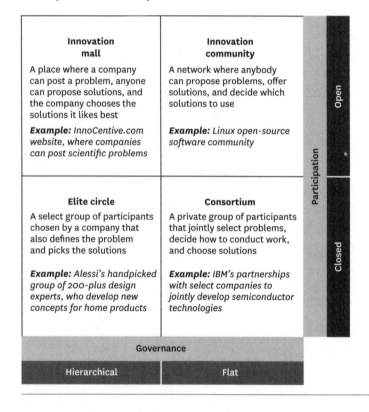

Innovation mall	**Innovation community**	**Open**
A place where a company can post a problem, anyone can propose solutions, and the company chooses the solutions it likes best	A network where anybody can propose problems, offer solutions, and decide which solutions to use	
Example: *InnoCentive.com website, where companies can post scientific problems*	**Example:** *Linux open-source software community*	**Participation**
Elite circle	**Consortium**	**Closed**
A select group of participants chosen by a company that also defines the problem and picks the solutions	A private group of participants that jointly select problems, decide how to conduct work, and choose solutions	
Example: *Alessi's handpicked group of 200-plus design experts, who develop new concepts for home products*	**Example:** *IBM's partnerships with select companies to jointly develop semiconductor technologies*	
Governance		
Hierarchical	Flat	

solvers is crucial. Closed modes, obviously, tend to be much smaller than open ones.

When you use a closed mode, you are making two implicit bets: that you have identified the knowledge domain from which the best solution to your problem will come, and that you can pick the right collaborators in that field. Alessi, an Italian company famous for the postmodern design of its home products, bet that postmodern architecture would be a fruitful domain for generating interesting product ideas and that it could find the best people in that field to work with. It invited 200-plus collaborators from that domain to propose product designs. If you don't know where to look for solutions or who the key players are (and have no way to find out), a closed mode like Alessi's elite circle is a dangerous shot in the dark.

The big advantage of an open network is its potential to attract an extremely large number of problem solvers and, consequently, a vast number of ideas. You do *not* need to identify either the best knowledge domains or the most appropriate experts in those domains. It's like throwing an open house party: You just make it known you are having a party and provide the right inducements, and (you hope) the right people will show up.

With open participation, you don't need to know your contributors. Indeed, the fact that you *don't* know them can be particularly valuable; interesting innovative solutions can come from people or organizations you might never have imagined had something to contribute. That is the concept behind Threadless.com, a largely online retailer of T-shirts, whose designs come from the masses. By operating an innovation mall where 600,000 members submit proposals for about 800 new designs weekly, Threadless gets a steady flow of unusual and singular ideas. (Mall members and visitors to the website vote on the designs, but the Threadless staff makes the final decision on which ones to produce and rewards their creators.)

Open modes, however, have their disadvantages. Notably, they're not as effective as closed approaches in identifying and attracting the best players. That's because as the number of participants increases, the likelihood that a participant's solution will be selected (especially for an ambiguous problem) decreases. The best parties, therefore, prefer to participate in closed relationships. Open modes work best when the spread between the ideal solution and the average solution is not big and the consequences of missing out on a much better solution from an elite player are small.

How to choose the best mode of collaboration

When selecting a mode of collaborative innovation, executives need to consider the distinct strategic trade-offs of each mode. Below are some important advantages and challenges of the different approaches to collaboration, and examples of capabilities, assets, processes, and kinds of problems that make each easier to carry out.

Advantage: You receive a large number of solutions from domains that might be beyond your realm of experience or knowledge, and usually get a broader range of interesting ideas.

Challenge: Attracting several ideas from a variety of domains and screening them.

Enablers: The capability to test and screen solutions at low cost; information platforms that allow parties to contribute easily; small problems that can be solved with simple design tools, or large problems that can be broken into discrete parts that contributors can work on autonomously.

Advantage: You receive solutions from the best experts in a selected knowledge domain.

Challenge: Identifying the right knowledge domain and the right parties.

Enablers: The capability to find unspotted talent in relevant networks; the capability to develop privileged relationships with the best parties.

		Participation	
Innovation mall	Innovation community		**Open**
Elite circle	Consortium		**Closed**
Governance			
Hierarchical	Flat		

Advantage: You control the direction of innovation and who captures the value from it.

Challenge: Choosing the right direction.

Enablers: The capability to understand user needs; the capability to design systems so that work can be divided among outsiders and then integrated.

Advantage: You share the burden of innovation.

Challenge: Getting contributors to converge on a solution that will be profitable to you.

Enablers: Processes and rules that drive parties to work in concert to achieve common goals.

Open modes are effective only under certain conditions. First, it must be possible to evaluate proposed solutions at a low cost. Sometimes the screening process is extremely cheap and fast. (For instance, it might be easy to assess whether a particular module of software code works or has bugs.) In other cases, though, the only way to find out whether an idea is worth pursuing is through expensive and time-consuming experiments, and you'll want to consider fewer (but better) ideas. The only way to do that is to invite contributions from the problem solvers that you think will have the best chance of providing good ideas. That is, to opt for a closed mode.

Consider the following simple but scary example. You have a serious illness, and you want to find the best possible treatment. Employing an open mode, you post your problem on the internet, ask for advice, and get 50 ideas that look interesting. But immediately, you face two issues. The first is what statisticians refer to as a sample selection problem: Are these the best 50 ideas out there? Maybe the most knowledgeable doctors are so busy treating patients that they don't participate in these forums, and only the doctors who have time on their hands (a bad sign for sure!) responded. The second issue is that you have to invest a lot of time and resources to evaluate the 50 ideas (visiting doctors and so on). Even worse, you may have only one shot at getting the right treatment. (Are you really going to "try out" more than one surgery?) That is why when confronted with a medical problem, we might do some research to identify elite specialists, pick one, and then seek a second opinion from one or two others.

Alessi is in a similar boat. Given the large population of designers, it could easily launch an open design competition for, say, a corkscrew on its website. With its high standing in the world of design, the firm would probably attract many proposals. However, it is not posing technical problems that have one or a few optimal solutions that can be clearly defined, thereby allowing contributors to screen many of their ideas themselves. Alessi is looking for concepts whose value is based on intangible properties such as aesthetics and emotional and symbolic content. Since there is no clear right or wrong answer, Alessi could receive thousands of proposals, creating a massive evaluation burden for the company. And because the company's strategy is to offer products with radical designs that anticipate market needs, its offerings often initially confuse consumers. Therefore it can't shift the evaluation burden to customers by asking them which designs they prefer, as Threadless does. That's why Alessi has to ensure that it will receive a few good ideas from a relative handful of contributors.

Another requirement of open modes is that participating in them must be easy. This is possible when a problem can be partitioned into small, well-defined chunks that players can work on autonomously at a fairly low cost. Someone creating a potential decoration for a Threadless T-shirt doesn't need sophisticated design infrastructure or knowledge of how the company will knit yarns or tailor shirts. The inherently modular structure of the Linux open-source community allows software developers to create code for new features without touching other parts of the application, which has more than four million lines of code. Over the past decade, such open collaboration has been made easier by information platforms that allow participants to make contributions, share work, and observe the solutions of others.

Of course, not all problems can be partitioned into small, discrete chunks. For example, the development of radically new product concepts or product architectures is an integral task that has to be embraced in its entirety. In such cases, closed modes that provide an environment where collaborators can closely interact must be employed. This is what led IBM to invite a handful of selected partners (including Siemens, Samsung, Freescale, Infineon, and STMicroelectronics) to join its Microelectronics Joint Development Alliance consortia for developing semiconductor technologies such as memory, silicon-on-insulator components, and chip-manufacturing processes.

Flat or Hierarchical Governance?

As discussed earlier, the chief distinction between a hierarchical and a flat form of governance is who gets to define the problem and choose the solution. In the hierarchical form, a specific organization has this authority, which provides it with the advantage of being able to control the direction of the innovation efforts and capture more of the innovation's value. In the flat form, these decisions are either decentralized or made jointly by some or all collaborators; the advantage here is the ability to share with others the costs, risks, and technical challenges of innovating.

Hierarchical governance is desirable when your organization has the capabilities and knowledge needed to define the problem and evaluate proposed solutions. Consider companies that post scientific problems on the innovation mall InnoCentive.com. The problems are generally smaller pieces of the sponsors' much larger R&D programs. These kingpins have a clear understanding of the relevant technologies and markets (user needs and functional requirements) and can define the system configuration and coordinate the work of various collaborators.

Conversely, flat modes work well when no single organization has the necessary breadth of perspective or capabilities. Look again at open-source software projects. These often develop very specific modules of code to address problems that users have encountered (a bug in an existing piece of code or the need for a specific hardware driver). In this case, the users are best positioned to devise and test solutions because they're closest to the problem. Indeed, they usually have discovered the problem in the first place. Or take IBM's microelectronics consortia. Since semiconductor companies other than IBM possessed critical knowledge, skills, and assets needed for microprocessor design, a hierarchical structure would have made no sense.

Flat modes are also appropriate when collaborators all have a vested interest in how a particular problem is solved and will participate only if they get some say in the decisions. For example, all the members of the IBM consortia formed over the years have expected to use in their own factories and product lines the technologies they develop collaboratively. For this reason, IBM and its partners chose a governance structure that provided each a strong voice in how the technology is developed.

Designing incentives—both financial and nonfinancial—that attract external collaborators is crucial with any of the four modes of collaboration. Nonfinancial rewards like high visibility in the job market, an enhanced reputation among a peer group, the psychological fulfillment of pursuing a strong interest, and the chance to use solutions in one's own business can replace or complement monetary rewards. There are no hard rules about which incentives work best with particular forms of collaboration. Although people often associate psychological fulfillment with innovation communities, it can be a powerful incentive in the other modes as well. For example, Alessi not only shares royalties from sales with the designers in its elite circle but also includes their names in product marketing and offers them a high degree of freedom in the design process.

A Matter of Strategy

Choosing a collaboration mode involves more than understanding the trade-offs. A firm must take into account its strategy for building and capturing value. And as the strategy evolves, the right mode of collaboration might change, too.

Consider the approach that Apple used in developing software for the iPhone and how it changed over time. A key part of Apple's business strategy (across all its products) has been to maintain the integrity of its systems. Indeed, one of the joys (and thus differentiators) of an Apple product is that everything—the machine's hardware, software, and peripherals—seems to work together so seamlessly. Historically, this kept Apple more oriented toward closed modes, where it could better control the components that influenced the user's experience. The company took that approach in developing the first generations of the iPhone as well and relied on elite circles to develop early applications for it.

However, once the iPhone was established, Apple faced the challenge of adding software functionality and applications that would fuel more growth. Our framework helps map out the various options Apple had. It could define the applications it thought would be useful (for example, a way to synchronize the iPhone with various mobile banking systems) and then engage the best software designers to develop them (the elite circle mode again). It could partition the development of particular applications into simple chunks and then go to a bazaar like TopCoder.com and tap hordes of software developers to write code for each chunk (the innovation mall mode). It could release a development package to third-party developers and let them define and create applications that would be useful (the innovation community mode). Or Apple could work jointly with a firm like Intuit to create mobile banking software (the consortium mode). Each of these modes could certainly generate new applications, but each would have a very different impact on the iPhone platform.

To stick with the elite circle mode, Apple needed to feel confident that it knew which applications customers would want and could identify the best partners for creating them. Given the huge variety of potential applications, Apple realized that there was no way that, either alone or with a small group of collaborators, it could anticipate all the applications that an iPhone owner might find useful or just fun. So it opted to encourage a thousand flowers to bloom and allow the market to decide which ones should be picked. This reasoning ruled out the elite circle, the consortium, and the innovation mall. Accordingly, Apple introduced a kit in March 2008 that allows a community of third-party developers to create applications based on the iPhone OS platform and provide them to users directly through the iPhone. (If an application is not free, the developers keep 70% of its revenues and Apple gets 30%.)

The rollout of mobile phones using Android, Google's operating system, could prompt Apple to adopt a two-part collaboration strategy. Since Android is open-source software, it may attract an even larger community of developers than the iPhone. So Apple might decide to supplement the applications developed by third parties with proprietary hardware features conceived by its own staff and created with the help of elite circles of hardware manufacturers. That illustrates another important point: Companies can use a combination of collaboration modes simultaneously to support their strategies.

IBM's successful use of *both* an innovation community and consortia to support the strategy of its server and mainframe computer businesses is an excellent real example. IBM's strategy is to compete on the basis of hardware differentiation and service. Toward that end, the company has striven to commoditize operating systems by embracing Linux and participating actively in the open-source community—one of the first major computer makers to do so. But to continue to differentiate its hardware, IBM needs to stay on the leading edge of microprocessor technology. Given the increasing scale required to keep up with the likes of Intel, IBM turned to its consortia of semiconductor companies, which have shared development costs. This combination of innovation approaches has allowed IBM to gain market share in an intensely competitive and dynamic market.

As IBM illustrates, a key component of strategy is exploiting a firm's unique assets and capabilities. In choosing one or more collaborative modes, a firm's senior managers therefore must ask: Which of our unique assets and capabilities are we trying to enhance the value of? And what's the best way to enhance it?

A firm's collaboration capability itself can be exploited for profit. InnoCentive.com, for example, is a spin-off of an innovation mall developed by Eli Lilly for internal purposes. Alessi is now leveraging the value of its connections with more than 200 designers by assisting companies in other businesses with product design. Alessi helps them identify the designers (usually from its own network) who can best address their specific needs. In return, Alessi receives royalties from sales of the resulting products—which now account for almost 30% of its revenues.

A New Source of Advantage

As with any strategic variable, collaborative approaches to innovation offer an array of choices and complex trade-offs. As the examples in this article suggest, each approach can be highly effective under the right conditions. Senior managers need to be wary of the notion that one type of collaboration is superior to others. Open is not always better than closed, and flat is not always better than hierarchical.

Developing an effective approach to collaboration starts with a solid understanding of your company's strategy. What is the business problem you want innovation to solve? Are you (like Alessi) trying to create a distinctive product that breaks boundaries? Are you (like IBM) trying to keep up with larger rivals (like Intel and Taiwan Semiconductor) in an intense technology race? Or are you (like Apple today) looking to broadly expand the applications of your product?

Companies must also ask what unique capabilities they bring to the collaborative process. Firms with deep relationships in a space, for example, are much better positioned to exploit an elite circle mode than a newcomer is.

It's not surprising, then, that differences in strategy and capabilities can lead to different kinds of collaboration networks competing against one another in the same industry. Thus, the task of senior leadership in innovation has broadened and become truly strategic. It is no longer just a matter of hiring the most talented and creative people or establishing the right internal environment for innovation. The new leaders in innovation will be those who can understand how to design collaboration networks and how to tap their potential.

Originally published in December 2008. Reprint R0812F

About the Contributors

HERMINIA IBARRA is a professor of organizational behavior and the Cora Chaired Professor of Leadership and Learning at Insead.

MORTEN T. HANSEN is a management professor at the University of California, Berkeley, School of Information, and at Insead.

DANIEL GOLEMAN is a cochairman of the Consortium for Research on Emotional Intelligence in Organizations at Rutgers University.

RICHARD BOYATZIS is the H. R. Horvitz Professor of Family Business and a professor in the departments of organizational behavior, psychology, and cognitive science at Case Western Reserve University.

JOHN ABELE cofounded Boston Scientific in 1979. Having retired from its board in May 2011, he now serves as director emeritus.

PAUL ADLER is a professor of management and organization at the Marshall School of Business of the University of Southern California, where he holds the Harold Quinton Chair in Business Policy.

CHARLES HECKSCHER is a professor at Rutgers University's School of Management and Labor Relations and director of the Center for Organizational Learning and Transformation.

LAURENCE PRUSAK is an independent consultant who teaches in the Information and Knowledge Strategy program at Columbia University.

RANJAY GULATI is the Jaime and Josefina Chua Tiampo Professor of Business Administration at Harvard Business School.

RICHARD MCDERMOTT is the president of McDermott Consulting and a visiting fellow at Henley Business School.

DOUGLAS ARCHIBALD is the director of Whole Education.

JEFF WEISS is an adjunct professor at the U.S. Military Academy at West Point and a partner at Vantage Partners, a Boston-based consultancy specializing in corporate negotiations and relationship management.

JONATHAN HUGHES is a partner at Vantage Partners.

ANDREW P. MCAFEE is a principal research scientist at the MIT Center for Digital Business.

GARY P. PISANO is the Harry E. Figgie, Jr., Professor of Business Administration at Harvard Business School.

ROBERTO VERGANTI is a professor of innovation management at the Politecnico di Milano, Italy.

Index

Abele, John, 31–43
accountability, 12
  collective, 86
  in conflict escalation, 104–105
Adler, Paul, 45–57
Advanced Instruments, 32, 36
affection, for leaders, 47, 48
agendas, 134
agility, 12
Akamai Technologies, 4–5
Alessi, 141, 143, 145–146, 150
alignment, 1–2
American Heart Association, 39
Anderson, Tim, 83
Android, 149
AOL, 49
Apple, 8, 141, 148–149
Archibald, Douglas, 79–89
architecture, collaborative, 137–138
assets, intangible, 118
attunement, 18, 20–21, 26
authoring, 119, 121–122
authority, 13. *See also* leaders and
    leadership
  in collaborative communities, 42
  customer focus and, 66–67
autonomy, 70
awareness, organizational, 18, 26

balloon catheters, 36–42
Bank of America, 64, 65
Becht, Bart, 7, 11
behavior
  mirroring, 17–20
  social intelligence and, 23
Benioff, Marc, 1–2
BenQ, 76
Best Buy, 60, 73
best-practice transfer, 133
"BlackBerry Beth" blog, 5
blogs, 5

Blue Cross and Blue Shield of
  Florida, 98–99, 100–101
Boston Scientific, 33, 36–38
boundary-spanning skills, 72–74
Bowlby, John, 29
Boyatzis, Richard, 15–29
brainstorming, 51
broadcast searches, 119, 121–122
Burke, Don, 122–123
business road maps, 51–52

capabilities
  collaboration types and, 151
  developing employee, 61, 62, 65,
    71–74
Capability Maturity Model, 45–46,
  50, 51
career paths, 73–74
Carlucci, Alessandro, 8–9
Cavallo, Kathleen, 23–26
centralization, participative, 55–56
Chambers, John, 66, 69
change agents, 41–42
Chatter, 1–2
Christensen, Clay, 32
Chrysler, 128, 131
Cisco Systems, 66, 68–69, 71
Citibank, 46, 49, 50, 53–54
coaching and mentoring
  conflict escalation and, 101–104
  for leaders, 9
  in social intelligence, 24–25
collaboration
  architecture for, 137–138
  benefits of, 91
  choosing the right kind of, 137–151
  communities in, 31–43, 45–57
  conflict and, 91–111
  connectors in, 3–6
  consensus versus, 10
  costs of, 127, 129, 132–134, 135–136

collaboration (*continued*)
 digital, 113–124
 diverse workforce and, 6–8
 governance and, 85, 138, 146–148
 informal networks and, 79–89
 initiatives for, 91–92
 in leadership teams, 8–11
 myths of, 94–95
 negative internal, 125–136
 during recessions, 133
 technologies for, 1–2, 42–43,
  88–89
 value destruction with, 131–134
 when to use or when not to use,
  125–136
collaboration penalties, 130
collaboration premiums, 129–130
collective intelligence, 119, 121–122
Combelles, Annie, 135–136
command-and-control leadership,
 10, 11
commoditization, 59–60
communication
 in conflict resolution, 97
 culture of cooperation and, 69–70
 social intelligence and, 24–26
communities
 balloon catheter design, 36–42
 building, 32, 45–57
 challenges facing, 56–57
 change initiative in, 52–54
 commitment to, 35
 documentation in, 54–55
 establishment bucking and, 38–39
 ethic of contribution in, 46, 49–51
 expectations for, 85–87
 exploitation in, 32
 face-to-face contact in, 88
 goals and deliverables for, 84–85
 governance of, 85
 infrastructure for, 46, 55–56
 innovation, 138, 142
 IT tools for, 88–89

 leadership training for, 87–88
 managing, 80, 85
 maximizing impact of, 87–89
 organizational structure for, 51,
  55–56
 ownership in, 53–54
 of practice, 79–89
 processes for, 46, 51–55
 purpose in, 46, 47–49, 56–57
 strategic setup for, 82–87
 teams compared with, 86
 time for participation in, 87
 vision for, 32, 46
communities of practice, 79–89
competitive advantage, 57, 150–151
Computer Sciences Corporation,
 45–46, 50, 51
Comstock, Beth, 5, 6
confidence, 39, 43
conflict, 91–111
 constructive, 12
 escalation of, 93, 101–104,
  104–109
 inevitability of, 92
 joint escalation of, 104–105
 learning from, 93, 109–111
 managing at point of, 92–93,
  96–104
 managing upon escalation, 93,
  104–109
 managing up the management
  chain, 101–104, 106–107
 resolution method for, 107–109
 resolution processes, 96–97
 trade-offs in resolving, 97–101,
  108
 value of, 7, 92–93
connections with external partners,
 61, 62, 65, 74–77
connectors, global, 3–6
ConocoPhillips, 88, 89
consensus, 10, 11, 12
consortia, 138, 142, 149–150

Consortium for Research on Emotional Intelligence in Organizations, 16
contribution, ethic of, 46, 49–51
cooperation, 61, 62, 64–65, 68–71
    conflict and, 92
    external partners and, 77
coordination, 61, 62–67
Corporate Solutions, 64–65, 67, 70–71
costs
    collaboration, 127, 129, 132–134, 135–136
    expected, 118
    opportunity, 127, 128–129, 131–132
crises, social intelligence in, 27–28
cross-selling, 133
cross-unit product innovation, 133
crowdsourcing, 138
culture
    of cooperation, 68–71
    external partnerships and, 75–76, 77
    shared, in communities, 50
curiosity, 39, 43
Customer Centricity University, 73
customer focus
    capability and, 61, 62, 65, 71–74
    connections with external partners and, 61, 62, 65, 74–77
    cooperation and, 61, 62, 64–65, 68–71, 77
    coordination for, 61, 62–67
    customer knowledge and, 77–78
    silo busting for, 59–78
customer segments, 73
Cyrus the Great, 12

Daimler, 128, 131
Danone, 6
Dasborough, Marie, 18–19

decision making, 51, 97
    about trade-offs, 97–101
    customer focus and, 66–67
decision rights, 12
del.icio.us, 122
Dell, 60
Det Norske Veritas, 126–129, 131–134
digital natives, 7–8
Disney, 69
disruptive innovation, 32, 34–35
diversity
    collaborative communities and, 43
    conflict and, 13
    engaging talent at the periphery and, 6–8
    social intelligence and, 22
DNV. See Det Norske Veritas
Dotter, Charles, 37
DuPont, 57
Durkheim, Émile, 46
Dweck, Carol, 9–10

E2.0. See Enterprise 2.0
Eli Lilly, 150
elite circles, 138, 142, 148–149
emergent social software platforms (ESSPs), 113–124
    benefits of, 114, 119
    close colleagues and, 121–122
    definition of, 116
    employee behavior in, 117–118
    encouraging participation in, 120–121
    evaluation of, 122–123
    features of, 114
    results from, 114–115, 124
    return on investment and, 118–120
    risks versus rewards of, 116–118

Emotional and Social Competency Inventory, 26–27
emotional intelligence, 16. *See also* social intelligence
empathy, 15–16, 18, 26
employees
    capability development in, 61, 62, 65, 71–74
    career paths for, 73–74
    customer focus and, 69
    development of, 18, 27
    in E2.0, 117–118
    generalist, 72–74
    informal networks of, 79–89
    interpersonal ties between, 121–122
    at the periphery, engaging, 6–8
Employees First, Customers Second (Nayar), 10
engagement process, 8–9
Enterprise 2.0, 113–124
    benefits of, 119
    close colleagues and, 121–122
    definition of, 113, 116
    encouraging participation in, 120–121
    evaluating, 122–123
    results in, 114–115, 124
    return on investment in, 118–120
    risks versus rewards in, 116–118
Ericsson, 5
e-Solutions, 48–49, 50, 51–52, 53–54, 55
ESSP. *See* emergent social software platforms (ESSPs)
establishment bucking, 38–39
ethic of contribution, 46, 49–51
evaluation
    360-degree reviews, 10, 23–24, 26–27, 56
    in collaborative communities, 56
    customer focus and, 70–71
    of E2.0, 122–123

social intelligence and, 18–19, 21, 23–24, 26–27, 28
    stress response to, 28
expectations, 85–87, 120
exploitation, 32

Facebook, 4. *See also* social media
face-to-face contact, 88
feedback, 18–19. *See also* evaluation
Fernández-Aráoz, Claudio, 16
financial recessions, 133
flaming, 117
Fluor, 81–82, 86–87, 89
Food and Nutrition Security Community, 84
Forrester Research, 113
Foursquare, 4
Frappuccino, 75
free-agent communities, 50, 51, 54. *See also* communities
freeform software, 116
Freescale, 146

GE Healthcare, 59–60, 62, 77–78
gender differences, 22
General Electric, 5, 6, 59–60
General Motors, 57
Generation Y, 7–8
Gillmor, Steve, 2
Gladwell, Malcolm, 3
global connectors, 3–6
goals
    for communities of practice, 84–85
    in E2.0, 120
    performance versus learning, 9–10
Goleman, Daniel, 15–29
Google, 149
governance, 85, 138, 146–148
group editing, 119, 121–122

Gruentzig, Andreas, 33, 37–42
Gulati, Ranjay, 59–78

Haas, Martine, 125, 131
Hansen, Morten, 1–13, 125–136
Hay Group, 22, 23
HCL, 8
Heckscher, Charles, 45–57
homogeneity, 6, 7
Hopkins, Margaret, 22
Hughes, Jonathan, 91–111
humility, 42, 43
humor, 20

Ibarra, Herminia, 1–13
IBM, 46, 48, 50, 57
    conflict management at, 102, 107,
        108–109
    external partners and, 76
    Market Growth Workshop, 107
    Microelectronics Joint
        Development Alliance, 141,
        146, 149–150
incentives. See rewards and
    incentives
individualism, 54
Infineon, 146
influence, 18, 27
infrastructure, 46, 55–56
InnoCentive.com, 141, 147, 150
innovation
    cross-unit product, 133
    disruptive, 32, 34–35
    imperative for, 57
innovation communities, 138, 142,
    149–150
innovation malls, 138, 142
inspiration, 18, 27
intangible assets, 118–120
Intel, 97
Intellipedia, 122–123

interdependent process
    management, 51–55
intranets, 117–118. See also networks
intuition, 20–21
iPhone, 141, 148–149

Jim Beam Brands, 75
Johnson & Johnson, 110–111
Jones Lang LaSalle, 61–62, 63–65,
    66–67, 70–71, 72, 74
Jones Lang Wootton, 63–65

Kaiser Permanente, 46, 48, 52–53
kaizen, 51
Kaplan, Robert, 118
Kelleher, Herb, 22
Kenny, David, 4–5
Kidder, Tracy, 56
Kidney Safety Council, 83
kingpins, 139, 140, 147
KLA-Tencor, 103–104
knowledge
    collaboration type and, 142–143
    customer focus and, 77–78
    E2.0 and, 121–122
    learning from conflict, 93, 109–111
    learning goals and, 9–10
    management, in communities
        versus teams, 86
    mobilization of in communities,
        55–56
Knowledge and Innovation
    Network, 80–81

language differences, 6
laughter, 20
leaders and leadership
    affection for charismatic, 47, 48
    attuned, 18, 20–21
    collaborative, 1–13

leaders and leadership (*continued*)
  in communities, 87–88
  communities and, 31–43
  conflict management and, 91–111
  cross-functional, 66
  engaging talent at the periphery and, 6–8
  as global connectors, 3–6
  loosening control and, 12–13
  as silo-colliders, 31–43
  skills for collaborative, 3
  social intelligence and, 15–29
  strong, 12, 13
  styles of compared, 11
  teams, collaboration in, 8–11
Lerner, Sandy, 69
Linux, 141, 146, 150

mad cow disease, 126–129, 131–132, 134–136
Madsen, Henrik, 134–135
Malloy, Ruth, 22
Mandela, Nelson, 123
Marx, Karl, 46
matrix structure, 55–56
McAfee, Andrew, 113–124
McDermott, Richard, 79–89
McKee, Annie, 21
McQuary, John, 86–87
Mead, Margaret, 33
Medi-Tech, 36
mentoring. *See* coaching and mentoring
metrics
  capability development and, 72–73
  customer focus and, 69, 71
  with E2.0, 118–120
  short-term, innovation and, 9–10
  of social intelligence, 25–28
Microsoft, 8
mirror neurons, 17–20, 28
mission. *See* vision

modeling, 42, 104–109
Monaco Media Forum, 5
mood contagion, 17, 20, 28. *See also* social intelligence
Motorola, 76
multidomain skills, 72–74

NASA, 6, 46
Natura Cosméticos, 8–9
Nayar, Vineet, 8, 10
networks. *See also* emergent social software platforms (ESSPs)
  encouraging participation in, 146
  expectations for, 85–87
  face-to-face contact in, 88
  focus on issues in, 82–84
  goals and deliverables for, 84–85
  governance of, 85, 138, 146–148
  informal, 79–89
  IT tools for, 88–89
  managing, 80
  maximizing impact of, 87–89
  membership in, 138, 139–146
  open versus closed, 138, 139–146
  strategic setup for, 82–87
neuroscience, social, 15–22
Nokia, 7
norms, 13, 24. *See also* values
Norton, David, 118

obsession, 39
opportunity costs, 127, 128–129, 131–132
organizational awareness, 18, 26
organizational structure
  for collaboration, 95, 137–138
  for collaborative communities, 46, 51, 55–56
  coordination for customer focus and, 62–67
  customer focus and, 69–71

E2.0 and, 114
matrix, 55–56
oscillator neurons, 21, 28

Parsons, Talcott, 46
participative centralization, 55–56
participatory meeting
management, 51
partners and partnerships
customer focus and connections
with, 61, 62, 65, 74–77
incentives for, 147–148
open versus closed networks and,
138, 139–146
Pedote, Roberto, 9
peer collaboration, 86
penalties, collaboration, 129
performance indicators, 9–10. *See
also* metrics
customer focus and, 70–71
social intelligence and, 25–28
Pfizer, 81, 82–83, 89
pinball theory of management, 56
Pisano, Gary, 137–151
platforms, 116. *See also* emergent
social software platforms
(ESSPs)
portfolio approach, 83
Prescient Digital Media, 113, 121
processes, 46, 51–55
conflict resolution, 107–109
screening, 145–146
process mapping, 51, 53–54
Prusak, Laurence, 45–57
purpose, for collaborative
communities, 46, 47–49, 56–57

quality, 68

rapport, 24
Raymond, Eric, 114

Reckitt Benckiser, 6–7, 11, 12
relationships
conflict management and, 93,
96–104
customer, 61, 62
external, managing, 75–77
reliability, 57
research, 84
resonance, 21
responsibility, collective, 86
return on investment, 118–120, 127,
128, 131, 150
rewards and incentives
collaboration encouraged with,
94–95
in communities, 32, 36, 56
for cooperation, 68
customer focus and, 69, 71
in E2.0, 120–121
for leader collaboration, 11
for network participation,
147–148
social intelligence and, 18–19
Riboud, Franck, 6

Sala, Fabio, 20
sales, 34–35
Salesforce.com, 1–2, 8
Samsung, 146
Sazaby, 75
Schlumberger, 80–81, 86, 87, 89
screening processes, 145–146
self-development, 9
self-interest, 47
self-organization, 119
Senning, Ake, 38
Serena Software, 124
Siemens, 146
silos
collaboration initiatives and, 92
colliding, 31–43
cooperation and, 68–71

silos (*continued*)
  customer focus and, 59–78
  functional or geographic versus
    customer, 63
  solutions focus and, 59–61
  swapping, 67
social intelligence, 15–29
  definition of, 16
  gender differences in, 22
  improving, 22–26
  metrics for, 25–28
  mirror neurons and, 17–20
  self-assessment in, 18–19, 23
  training in, 23–26
social media
  collaborative leaders and,
    1–13
  Enterprise 2.0 and, 113–124
  global connectors in, 3–6
Solectron, 76
Solution Exchange, 83–84, 86,
    87, 89
solutions, as strategic priority,
    59–61
Soul of a New Machine, The
    (Kidder), 56
Southwest Airlines, 22
spheres of influence, 55–56
spindle cells, 21
sponsors, 85
Standard Oil, 57
Stanford University Medical
    Center, 59
Starbucks, 74–76, 77
STMicroelectronics, 146
strategy
  collaboration type and, 138,
    148–150
  product versus solution focus in,
    59–61
  recessions and, 133
  trade-off selection and, 98–99,
    100–101

Strategy Maps (Kaplan and
    Norton), 118
stress responses, 28
suppliers, 74–77

Target, 69, 76
teams
  collaboration through, 94
  communities compared
    with, 86
  customer focus and, 66
  diversity in, 7–8
  leaders in directing, 12
  social intelligence and, 18, 27
Technicon, 33–36
Technicon Symposium, 35
Telus, 105
Threadless.com, 143, 146
360-degree reviews, 10, 23–24,
    26–27, 56
timelines, 118
time management, 87
Tipping Point, The (Gladwell), 3
TopCoder.com, 149
Torvalds, Linus, 41
Total Joint Dance, 52–53
trade-offs, 97–101, 108–109
  type of collaboration and, 137,
    139, 144
tradition, 47
training
  for community leadership,
    87–88
  for customer focus, 71–74
  in social intelligence, 23–26
transaction costs, 96–97
transparency, 10, 108–109
trust
  in communities, 36
  ethic of contribution and, 50–51
  face-to-face contact and, 88
Twitter, 4

United Nations Solution Exchange,
    83–84, 86, 87, 89
user groups, 35

values
    in collaborative communities, 46,
        49–51
    culture of cooperation and, 69–70
vendors, 74–77
Verganti, Roberto, 137–151
vested interests, 147
vision
    in communities, 32, 46
    for social intelligence, 23, 24
VistaPrint, 124

Wales, Jimmy, 41
Wal-Mart, 60
Warwick Business School,
    80–81
Warwick Innovative Manufacturing
    Research Centre, 80–81
Weber, Max, 46, 47
Weiss, Jeff, 91–111
Wells Fargo, 133
"What Makes a Leader?"
    (Goleman), 15
Whitehead, Jack, 33–36, 37, 42
Wikipedia, 122
Winnicott, D.W., 29
World Economic Forum, 5

Smart advice and inspiration from a source you trust.